AF264987

Marco & Mariposa

A NOVELLA

by
Freddy Bradburn and Marcy Lewis

Freddy

Marcy and I started writing together after we had been dating for awhile. The fact we are both writers and we were having to spend time away from each other prompted some long email exchanges. I then had the idea (Marcy will claim it was her idea) that we begin writing stories together. What occurred became this lovely Friday night ritual. We alternated writing weekly chapters. Marcy would fix us a cocktail and then one person would read their new chapter to the other person. We did this for a couple of years and five or six novellas later, we have decided to publish the first (and probably our favorite) of our novellas. It is fable. We love it very much and hope you will like it too.

Thanks to Todd Buckner, our friend, neighbor, and my long time bandmate for the book design and the illustrations.

Freddy

Marcy

Some time ago, when Bradburn and I were still great friends but not yet romantically involved, he suggested we collaborate on some sort of writing project. He was vague but hopeful about this. I wasn't sure how to respond, because of his vagueness and because of the fact that he was a songwriter and I wrote fiction. How shall we mix that? Nothing more was done until about a year later when I was having coffee with my friend Amy and she told me about a writing project she was collaborating on where she and her friend handed the manuscript back and forth, writing alternating chapters. I loved this idea, and I knew right away that I was going to steal it. At this point, two things had changed since Bradburn's original suggestion—first, we were now dating, seeing each other on weekends, and second, he had sent me a piece of fiction he'd written, a fable about a sweet little tadpole and a monarch butterfly. In his story, the butterfly was a proper school marm, but pretty. I decided to give her a little sass, and wrote a follow-up chapter wherein she implores "her little slug" to kiss her. I surprised Bradburn with the chapter the following weekend. We continued to exchange chapters, and it became a kind of language between us. It is a story about the mismatched love of a tadpole and a butterfly, but it is also the story of our falling in love in real-life—two stories about unlikely love and the beautiful surprises such an arrangement can bring.

Marcy

Published by Freddysongs

©2018 Freddysongs
First Edition: June 2018
Printed in USA
Book design by Eckenrod Studio.
Illustrations by Ozmoid.
Cover by Piffle Press.

Authors: Bradburn, Freddy; Lewis, Marcy
Title Marco & Mariposa, first edition
ISBN: 978-0-692-12562-5

A hopping good read...
Charlie "Crick" Cricket

I liked the sex...
Pig in a Poke

Devil of a good story...
Jack Rabbit

I give it five stars...
The Big Dipper

Marco & Mariposa

A NOVELLA

by
Freddy Bradburn and Marcy Lewis

Mariposa: Beginnings

When you've begun life as a tiny white caterpillar, of voracious appetite and squishy form, and you spend your adolescence in a lightless little cocoon and you emerge, finally uncramping your skinny black legs and unsticking your new papery wings, you might discover you're beautiful. You might. You might be happy for a moment, catching your reflection in a pond or a puddle or someone's darkened kitchen window. You might stand there awkwardly, trying to get a look at your backside, your best feature. The light might catch your wings just so, and oh glory. The orange of your wings is the purest orange in all of nature. You are the Queen of Metamorphosis. A lesson in changing, in evolving, for us all. Hope that a crummy, hungry childhood, that time spent in the dark, in the quiet, steeped in loneliness, that all of this will be so worth it. Change is good. The change is coming. Hearken. Be sweet and long-suffering, and above all, above all: be of good cheer.

Believe: all will be beautiful. You are. You are a butterfly.

You might give yourself a name. Let's try Mariposa. It means butterfly in Spanish. This makes sense: all Monarchs dream of Mexico. You do. You believe in Mexico. Even though you live here, in this pond. This pond, full of horse flies and algae and great, ugly, burping frogs.

You believe in yourself. You believe in your good looks.

You are so beautiful, you decide to turn yourself into a star. The brightest star in the sky. You are the first to sign up for karaoke every Saturday night at the Chicken or Egg Pub. You're Aretha Franklin. A natural woman.

You're also a school teacher. You teach the brats; this pays the bills. You throw your crummy, pond scum-sucking boyfriend to the curb. You decide your very provincial mother knows nothing. You wait for something better. You wait for stardom to strike. You wait for all of your beautiful butterfliness to bring you whatever it is it's supposed to bring you. What will it bring you?

You sing, R-E-S-P-E-C-T. Find out what it means to me.

You fly home alone, low to the ground, dodging cattails and little crops of monkey grass. You light on a midnight trumpet flower, turn your eyes to the dark sky. You let the moonlight bathe your wings.

You drink a Vodka-milkweed martini. You smoke Luckys.

You take the stage. Accept the microphone. The music begins and you follow the words on the screen. You open your butterfly mouth, stretch your wings, orange and glorious and spanning nearly four and a half inches. All the insects of pondland are there, waiting. Waiting for you, Miss Mariposa.

You say a little prayer. You never loved a man. You are rollin' in the deep.

The music fills you, spills out. You are poisonous, alive, the most beautiful now, in the last stage of your life. Your final metamorphosis.

Sing, Miss Mariposa, fucking sing.

Butterfly Out of Season

One intolerably muggy-buggy July afternoon, Miss Mariposa, relentless grammarian and occasional cloud-gazer, packed up her teacher bag at the end of the school day and flew off toward home. Her bag, which contained a bundle of ungraded essays and several bottles of bourbon-infused nectar—hey, she would say to anyone who raised an eyebrow, don't judge; you try teaching a gaggle of pond creatures how to diagram sentences—was too heavy and so her flight was wobbly and labored and dipped dangerously low at times. She veered sharply to avoid crashing into a dandelion stalk only to find herself flying straight into a stand of cattails. How did those get there? Once again, Miss Mariposa, burdened with such a heavy, clinking load, leaned away, narrowly missing disaster.

It was a dangerous life, she mused bitterly to herself. Miss Mariposa sighed. It was not a dangerous life. Not even a little bit. The thought—how very un-dangerous her life was—made her want to drop to the grass and down one of her bottles of bourbon-infused nectar before she even made it home. This was how sad she was, how full of career frustration and general butterfly angst.

Miss Mariposa was two weeks old, middle-aged in butterfly years.

She lived in a scratchy yellow thicket of goldenrod and daylilies with a swarm of other butterflies; single girls like herself. Her thicket stood near the pond where she taught but not too near. One had to keep a certain distance between pupil and teacher. One should be, Miss Mariposa had learned in her education classes, friendly but not too familiar.

Recently, her thicket had been overrun by bumble bees. They were loud and buzzy and Miss Mariposa was annoyed. She'd heard them in her butterfly sleep; they'd thwarted her dreams. The buzzing made her antennae pulse unpleasantly.

She flew, wobbly and despondent, toward her home. But she didn't want to get there.

The trouble was every night could not be Karaoke night. Miss Mariposa loved Karaoke night, Saturdays at the Chicken or Egg Pub. She always wore her white go-go boots so she could pretend to be Nancy Sinatra though she had these horrible spindly butterfly legs, useless for anything other than pollen transfer. The boots may be made for walking, but Miss Mariposa could hardly get them to stay on her fragile stick legs.

A butterfly is more than a vehicle for pollen, her mother, a famous author and feminist-butterfly used to tell her. A butterfly needs a flower like a fish needs a bicycle, she said, and insisted Miss Mariposa fly off to college, but then derided her for choosing a career in education. You could have been anything, her mother lamented.

Anything. Miss Mariposa considered this. When she had been very young, so far into the other direction of who Miss Mariposa was now, she wasn't truly Mariposa at all yet, she had been visited by a vision: something great and orange and so purely itself it nearly folded in on itself and became something else. An orange cloud. A dream. She was, at the time she spied the vision, very young. Pre-pupa. Pre-self. Worm-like. (Never say worm, her mother, her aunts, her own father would say, if they were here, flying with her, listening in on her thoughts. Caterpillars are not worms, they would say; but, two things: 1. They were not, in fact, here. Miss Mariposa, in her quest to find herself, had severed, or nearly severed, all ties to her family—she still thought of them though, and argued with them, silently inside her mind, all the time. And, 2. She had been a worm, in the sense that we were all worms long, long ago. This is both evolutionarily true, though arguable, and true in the sense that all matter is recycled; these carbon atoms have been shifting, creature to creature, for a very, very long time.)

And, besides: caterpillar, worm. Wasn't it all the same?

And, besides: she was speaking metaphorically. Or perhaps, developmentally. She had been a worm, unformed. Not yet her.

And yet. And yet. That vision, something orange and alive and cloudlike and real, stayed with her, incarnation to incarnation. Worm to caterpillar to cocooned creature-in-transition to young butterfly to—as she was now, sigh—middle-aged butterfly. She couldn't access it, exactly, couldn't name it. But, still, it was there, just out of grasp: the orange cloud.

Orange, like a kumquat. Like the desert. Like a certain, rare jungle orchid.

All were things Miss Mariposa had never seen.

After nearly colliding with yet another stand of cattails—where had they come from and why did they keep sprouting up, even though she was flying away from the pond?—Miss Mariposa, who was thinking and not thinking of the vision of orange she'd had in her pre-pre-larvae state, decided she would absolutely not go home tonight and instead landed on the tiniest little sprig of periwinkle. It was out of season; this was the strangest pond-land in the world. Nothing made sense here, which was the only reason Miss Mariposa could stand it at all. She settled back, leaning against a moss-covered stone, and drank. The sky grew dark. She watched the stars until one slid across the sky and disappeared. She knew it was dropping into a faraway ocean. It would turn into a starfish while Miss Mariposa was stuck here, drinking alone on a non-Karaoke night, still unwilling to go home.

"Excuse me? Miss Mariposa?" This was a voice from the darkness, and then there was the stirring of weeds, and a tiny green creature emerged, into the scant silvery starlight. "Umm, I saw you sitting here, alone, and I just wanted to check. Are you alright?"

It was Marco Tad Polo. He was a pupil from Miss Mariposa's cloud-diagramming class, a tadpole who seemed to be stuck there in early tadpolehood. He had been a member of Miss Mariposa's class for eight days now and had not sprouted a single limb-bud. But he was sweet. Miss Mariposa knew that he had a crush on her; he tried to hide his feelings but he smiled broadly and blushed greenly and pretended to love cloud-diagramming.

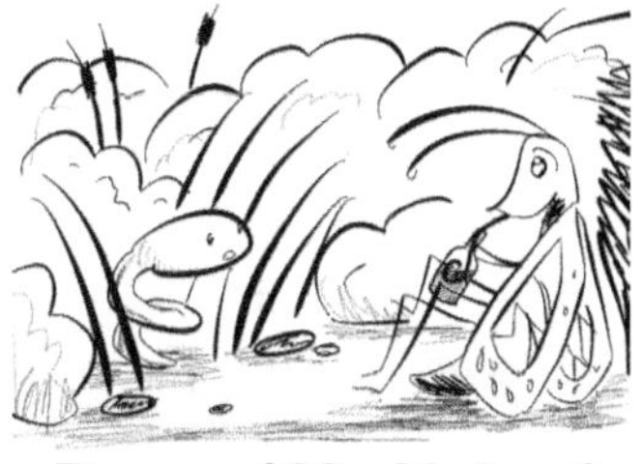

Excuse me? Miss Mariposa?

"Oh," she said. "Marco." She smiled at him. It was late and her head was a little swimmy from the bourbon-nectar, her bottle nearly empty, and despite herself—the fact that she was his teacher—Miss Mariposa found the tadpole charming. Frankly sexy. He was so green, so beautifully speckled, with such a fluttery little tail. (Another wonder of this very strange pond-world, how the very aptly gilled Marco Tad Polo, hopping about on his tail, curved like a spring beneath him, existed on dry land.) This was a dangerous situation, indeed, but Miss Mariposa found herself leaning forward, her butterfly chin resting in her butterfly palm.

"Miss Mariposa? Are you alright?"

He was a very good little tadpole. Unerringly polite, respectful of his elders. He pretended not to notice the drunken sway in Miss Mariposa's step as she stood up, slowly and with great care, and approached him.

"Have you ever wondered what happened to Nancy Sinatra?" she asked.

"Ma'am?"

"Goddamnit, Marco-fucking-Tad-fucking-Polo, do not call me ma'am!"

Oh dear, the butterfly thought: maybe the spiked nectar was getting to her more than it ought. Poor Marco looked afraid, quivering and pale green.

"I'm sorry, Marco, I'm so very sorry." She hiccupped. "I don't know what got into me. I'm just too young for that ma'am business. Do you know how old I am?" And then, before he could answer, she told him. "I'm fourteen days old."

"Oh." Marco Tad Polo didn't know what to say. He, the perpetual tadpole, never thought about age.

"A fortnight," the butterfly continued, as if suddenly remembering she was an English teacher. "I emerged from my cocoon a mere two weeks ago. And now look at me." She hiccupped again and reached for her bag. "Where," she asked, "did I put that extra bottle of nectar?" She was speaking aloud but not really talking to anyone. Marco Tad Polo stood back, waiting.

"Miss Mariposa, I hate to see you so, uh, upset. Is there anything I can get you?"

Miss Mariposa stopped scrounging around in her bag. She thought for a second, fluttered a bit closer to Marco. "Can you take me to New York?" She came still closer. "I want to try to make it on Broadway."

She was not expecting a yes from Marco. She landed on a soft bit of dirt, very close to Marco. Close enough to make out the tiny green pores in his green, green face. Despite herself, she found herself wishing he would kiss her. He smelled wonderful, like algae growing in the sunshine. Miss Mariposa closed her eyes. Please, she thought. Come on, Marco-fucking-Tad-fucking-Polo. Kiss me, she silently begged.

"All right."

Miss Mariposa blinked, surprised. "All right?"

"I will take you to New York."

"Oh. New York. I mean, you will? But, how? It's too long to hop or fly, at least without an actual airplane." But the butterfly, thoroughly soused, was intrigued. She threw her head back and sang, "You make me feel like a natural woman."

"I thought you were channeling Nancy Sinatra."

Miss Mariposa shrugged. "It comes and goes. All kinds. Later, we'll probably hear from Cher."

'I'll look forward to that,' Marco said, and made a gesture that might have looked like a man offering a woman his arm, but Marco didn't have an arm. Miss Mariposa instead wrapped one spindly butterfly-limb around the tadpole's thick and slimy neck.

'All right,' she said. This was dangerous, indeed. But the very thought—the fear over the danger she was stepping her dainty little, nectar-tasting butterfly legs into—felt distant. Harmless. Miss Mariposa was drunk and fearless. "Where are we going?" she asked.

The tadpole sighed. His features were merely little slits on his slick tadpole skin. "I just said. New York. So you can sing on Broadway." Miss Mariposa heard the impatience in his voice. It was such work, taking care of a drunken butterfly.

"All right," Miss Mariposa said at last, "let's go." She squeezed his neck. Of course, she didn't have any hope that he would actually do it, take her to New York, but she let him lead her through the weeds. Above them, the sky had turned so very black, the stars were extra bright by comparison. "Dazzling," the butterfly said, leaning into Marco Tad Polo. She closed her eyes. "I can still see them," she said, and hiccupped again. She laughed.

"Right this way," the tadpole said, and hurried her away from the not-dangerous-enough but very strange pond world. "Let's go," he whispered into her tiny ear, and Miss Mariposa fluttered her wings in anticipation.

Marco and the Pole of the Tad

Marco stood (or he sort of stood). He was a slitherer but he slithered as seductively as he could until he was right in front of the beautiful, if somewhat foul-mouthed, Mariposa. He pulled his little body as upright as he could.

"Would you like to kiss me, Marco?"

"Yes, I would."

Saying it was the easy part. Marco had not kissed anything before. Sure, he had practiced by kissing Algae, but it was a wet, slimy kiss that the Algae called French kissing. Marco did not know much about butterfly anatomy, except he knew it was complicated. And it appeared Mariposa was complicated in other ways as well. He wasn't sure how a butterfly kissed, so he stood upright and puckered his little tadpole lips and tried not to go into shy, nervous convulsions right away. Mariposa grabbed poor Marco with about four of her legs and laid one big kiss on him. If he thought the Algae was a wet kisser, this was a whole new experience. Think about it: do you know how long a butterfly's tongue is? She got into Marco's mouth and unrolled her tongue until it almost came out the other end of Marco. Marco could not believe how good it felt, partially because Mariposa had consumed a lot of bourbon-infused nectar, some of which was stored on her tongue. So Marco experienced the first pangs of love and sex, and impossible longing and got drunk all at the same time.

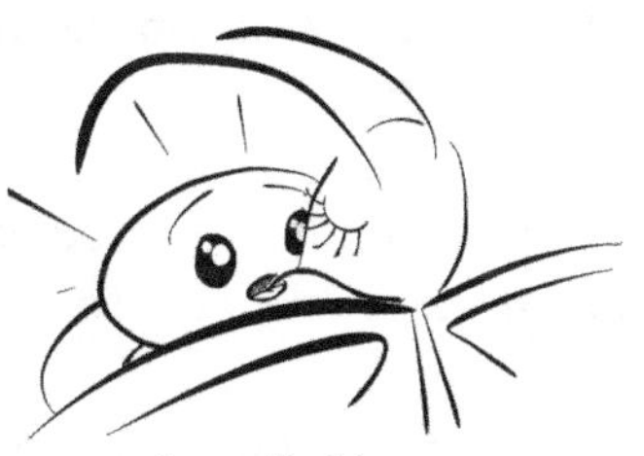

...and unrolled her tongue...

Mariposa suddenly pulled away a little and rolled in her tongue. "Why Marco, I think you've sprouted a leg suddenly."

"That's not my leg, ma'am, I mean Miss Mariposa." Marco blushed a near neon green. He was trying to be discreet but all of a sudden he looked like a flashing green billboard.

"So it's true what they say about 'the pole, the pole of the tad."

Marco had no idea what was going on. He was trying to keep up because it sure felt good. "Rub my antenna with your pole, Marco." Marco did his best to comply. It was tricky, working with an appendage of his body he'd never before known existed.

"Yes, yes, like that. Now harder, harder." Mariposa was fluttering her wings and screaming in a very high pitched voice, and Marco was squirming uncontrollably, stroking her antennae while flashing neon green. Marco knew the pond would be all abuzz with the gossip tomorrow, but he didn't care. What were the chances a tadpole would make love to a butterfly? That a tadpole could make love to a butterfly? It was just as he suspected: he loved her. He loved her. They would fly off to New York together. Of course, Marco had no clue what or where New York was. It must be on the other side of the pond somewhere. If it were on dry land, he might have to wait until he transformed into a butterfly (Yes, poor Marco believed tadpoles turned into butterflies).

"Yes! Yes! Yes!" Mariposa screamed. "Harder! Harder!"

Marco had never felt like this before. He looked at her shapely thorax. He was in an erotic garden few creatures got to experience. Oh spiders and bees sometimes experienced this ecstasy but then they were immediately devoured by their female counterparts. Oh and Preying Mantis too, but they were Jesus freaks so that was different. Marco suddenly looked around just to make sure he wasn't going to meet a similar fate. He was unsure what Mariposa saw in him. After all, he was just a Tadpole. Just a level up from slime. But maybe Mariposa was one of those females who liked to get down and dirty, or maybe she was attracted to his innocence or his intellectual curiosity. You didn't find much intellectual curiosity in the world of insects. Best just to enjoy this, whatever this was.

"Yes! Yes! Yes! Marco, you're amazing."

Mariposa had become suddenly very positive, Marco thought. Yes, he was amazing, he thought, at least for a larvae, a larvae in love, larvae diem. Suddenly, Marco felt the rush of feeling just before his tadpole orgasm and it shot him backward two feet into a puddle of water, which Marco was grateful for, because he had become dehydrated during insect sex. Mariposa came over and drank from the puddle and cuddled with Marco and she offered him a cigarette. Marco had never smoked but this was a day of firsts and he wasn't going to stop now.

The next day, just as Marco had predicted, the pond was abuzz with gossip. "A tadpole with a butterfly? Disgusting. Outrageous."

"And her so much older, and his teacher. She should be fired. The pole lice should be notified."

"Inter-species dating cannot be allowed. What would their children be? Slugs with wings, or worse, frogs with wings?"

Marco figured that, in a pinch, Mariposa could fly them to New York, if she were still interested when sober. She would certainly be in trouble. She would certainly be fired from her job. And after all, Marco wanted to travel, and he didn't weigh that much. He would be like a piece of carry-on luggage. His only reservation was that Mariposa was a terrible flyer. Even when sober, she flew too fast and erratically. Once she took four of them on a field trip and she nearly killed them all. Swerving in and out of traffic, just barely missing Cattails and Dogwoods, and when they reached their destination all the kids, including Marco, threw up.

But Marco always looked at the positives. It would be a great adventure, and perhaps he could serve as co-pilot and guide Mariposa when she flew a little recklessly. Marco had made up his mind. He would go with the beautiful Mariposa.

Butterfly in Decline

Mariposa shuddered through the last of her orgasms, which were considerable, both in intensity and in number, and reached for her student, who had slumped ungracefully into a mud puddle after his own tremulous and curiously bright orgasm. Miss Mariposa had never seen a creature glow more greenly—almost electrically—than the young and eager Marco Tad Polo. She discovered, to her surprise, that she was no longer drunk. Her head didn't swim and her limbs felt firmly and soberly connected to her. When she opened her mouth to speak, her words didn't slur.

"You're amazing," she said, nuzzling her pupil's slimy green neck. She drank deeply from the puddle and reached for her teacher bag. "Cigarette?"

They lounged in their puddle for some time. Marco was clearly new to smoking—he was clearly new to a lot of things—and he puffed tentatively while Miss Mariposa drew the smoke deep into her butterfly lungs and felt both fully alert and extraordinarily, wonderfully subdued. She sighed contentedly and murmured, "Goddamn, Marco. I'm so fucking happy." She exhaled a long plume of smoke. "What have you done to me," she asked, with affection, "you miserable little slug?"

But this happiness, if wholly different, better even than the kind of happiness she felt while she was on the karaoke stage, singing her little drunken butterfly heart out, was, like karaoke-happiness, not without its drawbacks.

"Oh, Marco, what will we do when you complete your metamorphosis and hop away?"

The poor tadpole looked confused by this and Miss Mariposa worried for a second that the boy was plain stupid. But if there was one advantage to living a long and lazy caterpillar life, full of eating and dozing and dreaming—her half-forgotten dream of something orange and soothing—and then, a long, dark cocoon-hibernation, filled with more dreaming, more painful existential contemplation while budding wings grew from her back with small, painful eruptions, while her squishy caterpillar body hardened into the slim and shapely insecty body of a butterfly, it was that you understood the difference between stupidity and naiveté. Stupid could be fixed, or at least improved upon, while naiveté could only be tarnished. Corrupted.

So instead of explaining the many changes his body would experience in its long and awkward trudge toward adulthood, the fully mature—the aging—butterfly kissed Marco again, long and hard. She once again made full and exultant—when had she screamed like that?—use of his young and ever-ready erection, which had popped out at her barely a third of the way into the kiss, and they fell again together into the puddle. Once again recovering from her various ecstasies, she began to lay out for him her plan.

"Listen," she whispered into the smooth and slimy spot of skin where, if he were a different sort of pond creature, his ears would be, "there will be talk tomorrow. Lots of talk. People don't understand," she hesitated, "love." Love. She was quiet a moment, more sober than ever before. She'd confessed her feelings for the slippery little tadpole and was surprised by the force of the word on her own tiny heart, deep inside her hard black exoskeleton. She did, oh, she did! She loved this sweet, naïve tadpole. "They won't understand it, Marco, our love for each other, and so they will try to tear us apart. They will be jealous and small-minded and judgmental, and they will want to fire me...or worse. Marco, listen to me. We can't let that happen."

The next day, it was just as Miss Mariposa had feared. All of pond-world was a'twitter with accusations and speculations. Miss Mariposa's immediate termination was called for. An official investigation was demanded. Many of her pupils' mothers kept their little ones home from school the next day, fearing what all the predatory butterfly might do to their meek and delightful offspring. If that horrible old butterfly whore will seduce a tadpole, one mother, a junebug, lamented, just imagine what she'll do to my little one. We simply cannot stand for this, she said.

...accusations and speculations.

This information was brought to them by Marco's brother Larry—Marco, being a tadpole, had approximately eleven thousand siblings—who further cautioned them: the mothers were organizing.

Miss Mariposa was furious they had called her old, and thoroughly insulted by several pond creatures' speculations as to what sort of creature might result from this sort of interspecies breeding.

"Really," she said, "I am a responsible butterfly, a grownup. I know how to protect myself from unplanned spawning."

"It's a good thing," Marco reminded her, "that we have a plan."

This reminder had the desired effect, and Mariposa calmed down. "Yes, our plan," she said. She thanked Larry, then dismissed him with a flutter of her wings. She dropped a kiss on Marco's cheek. She whispered, "Are you sure about this? About flying off to Broadway with me? You might never get to return to this pond." She looked around her disdainfully—she hated this place—but she knew leaving would be a big step for a little tadpole. Tadpoles don't travel like butterflies do. This was Marco's home; it was the only place he knew.

But Marco was a brave tadpole, and adventurous. "Absolutely," he said.

"Let's fly away together. I'm ready."

They left during the night. At first, everything went perfectly. Mariposa easily lifted Marco and he arched his little tadpole back in such a way that reduced drag and made him as sleek and aerodynamic as a tadpole could be. Mariposa was pleased; Marco Tad Polo, a thinker, a dreamer, and the most cooperative of all her students. Yes, yes, she had chosen the right student to corrupt.

Traveling to New York required Miss Mariposa to fly north rather than south, which went against her butterfly instincts, but, as she explained to young Marco, sometimes going against your instincts is exactly what a creature must do. Necessary, she said, but scary, too. It can be very scary, to go against what you feel you are supposed to be in order to become who you really, really—deep inside—are.

Marco Polo agreed. "Downright terrifying," he said.

It was an amazing thing to have a fellow creature understand you and Mariposa, once again experiencing the electrifying bolt of love, pointed her antenna even higher in the sky—they were already flying much higher than Monarchs usually dared—and together, she and Marco pushed through the clouds.

"The higher we go, the faster we'll get there," Miss Mariposa, who was never completely not a teacher, explained to Marco. "This has something to do with the theory of relativity and time travel," she said.

The first thing she'd told him, about flying higher in order to get there faster, she was pretty sure was true, but now she was just making shit up. But, she was a butterfly in love with a tadpole, trying to push right through the earth's atmosphere, to break through, into black space. What did it matter if she made perfect sense? Who cared? Life was too, too good in this moment to worry about making sense.

"I'll write a paper," Miss Mariposa said. "For the Love of Einstein: a Butterfly's Space Mission."

"Okay," Marco said. He yawned. It was way past his bedtime. "I would love to read that paper. Just don't make me diagram any of the sentences in it." He yawned again. He slumped a little, unable to hold to his rigid aerodynamic shape.

"Marco, it's all right. Go to sleep."

And then, Miss Mariposa began to sing. This was an unusual experience for her—singing while sober—but, for Marco, she did it. She sang a lullaby, and it sounded horrible. Miss Mariposa, for all of her love of karaoke, of making it big on Broadway, had never considered what she really sounded like. Her normal speaking voice was sweet and chirpy, but when she began to sing, her voice struggled to reach octaves no insect, not even a katydid, should attempt. She sounded like a half-strangled squirrel. Like a cawing crow with lungs full of helium. Like a thousand fingernails on a thousand chalkboards, but amplified and extra-warbly.

Marco winced. Fuck, he thought. (Miss Mariposa had corrupted him, turned him into a potty-mouth, if only in his thoughts.) This bitch sounds awful. He sighed inwardly, silently. He would have to find another talent for Miss Mariposa to showcase. They would never make it on Broadway, whatever that was, with this kind of voice.

Marco, shocked awake by the horrible screeching of his butterfly teacher, squirmed. Mariposa, unprepared for his sudden and somewhat violent twitching, faltered. The two dipped, and then, just as Mariposa was struggling to right them, up roared a great solar wind, which had gathered strength and blew, unhampered, a very long way through black space. The wind was charged and magnetic and otherworldly, and invisible. It found a tiny fissure in the earth's atmosphere, shot through miles of blue, and scorched the butterfly. It was a sudden heat in her left wing so hot, it felt cold—a kind of deep and sickening blue cold. Blue, like the hottest part of a flame, like ice frozen past its usual white.

My God, it was torn. Her wing was torn.

What little directional sense the usually-drunken butterfly had possessed was completely eradicated from her tiny butterfly brain in that terrible hot-cold pain, in the terrible knowledge that her wing was torn, and there's no greater injury for a butterfly, physical or otherwise. She could not even tell which direction was up. For the moment, she forgot there was such a thing as up or down or anything else.

Her wing was torn. She couldn't fly; she couldn't be. Couldn't exist at all. After all, what was a butterfly without the flying part?

She knew it would come to this. She had always known it had come to this. This was what a butterfly got for dreaming. For attempting to escape her tiny little butterfly life.

And she was bringing the tadpole with her. Her sweet, slimy Marco.

Where now was the great orange dream? Her kumquat dream, her hazy orchid. Now, Miss Mariposa knew: such things didn't exist.

The two spiraled downward, through the dizzying blue, faster and faster as they fell.

Marco and the Great Adventure

Marco took the cigarette from Mariposa. She had lit it off her lit cigarette and handed it to Marco. Well, she didn't really hand it. She put it in his mouth. He drew the smoke into his little lungs (or gills, whatever) and then proceeded to cough loudly.

"Easy, Marco." Mariposa said, cuddling into Marco. The cigarette made him feel like a firefly, you know, light-headed. He held the cigarette in his lips and Mariposa would take it out and flip the ashes. He could not believe he had made love to Mariposa, or really, she had made love to him. He was in love with her, of course, and he would follow her anywhere. Even though he knew this was probably a bad idea. But he was a male and he couldn't help it. He felt like he was maturing even as he lay there and felt the beauty and warmth of Mariposa's body against his. He felt two tiny hairs sprouting above his little lips so he was pretty sure he was growing a mustache. He also felt something inside him, on his sides, pressing against his skin. Maybe those were his wings. He had certainly been surprised by his penis and how Mariposa screamed and squirmed in delight, but he was pretty sure he wasn't going to have three penises. But with Mariposa he might need three.

As they lounged, Marco's mind wandered. He had always dreamed of transforming into a butterfly, and someone told him once that a tadpole transformed into a butterfly, and Marco believed it because he wanted to, and Marco was a dreamer. His brother Larry had laughed at him and told him, "No, we become great big frogs." He had about 10,000 brothers and sisters, and approximately 100 were named Larry, so he didn't give Larry's views much credibility. Marco believed you could become what you dreamed if you tried hard enough. The fact that he had just made love to a butterfly was proof, wasn't it? He might be the first tadpole ever to make love to a butterfly. Anything was possible. And by making love with a butterfly, then wasn't it possible he would acquire some butterfly genetic material in their transmission? But Mariposa had mentioned something about him maturing and hopping away. He actually remembered her words exactly, "Oh Marco, what will we do when you complete your metamorphosis and hop away?" He was confused by this. He was in denial. He looked at Mariposa blankly as she said this.

But really what did she know? She was exotic and beautiful and sexy, but she did say "fuck" a lot and she smoked and drank and seemed a bit unstable. But what if he did transform into a frog? Even if he had a cool mustache, he would still be a frog. What if those were arms poking at his sides? Well, he'd just have to wait and see. If he had arms he could hold Mariposa and really make love to her, at least, as long as he was still tadpole-like, a cute tadpole, but with arms, and he could learn to play the guitar like he always wanted, and write songs for Mariposa to sing. Perhaps he could find some mushroom or something that could halt the frog turning process.

Mariposa woke Marco from his reverie.

"They won't understand it, Marco, our love for each other, and so they will try to tear us apart. They will be jealous and small-minded and judgmental, and they will want to fire me…or worse. Marco, listen to me. We can't let that happen."

"No, no we can't," is all Marco said.

Things were happening fast. He wanted to be a tadpole of some renown, like his namesake, and here was his chance. He felt a deep, tadpolian love for Mariposa, deeper than any tadpole had ever felt, and he would go with her, even though he knew there would be trouble ahead. Lots of trouble.

The next night they were ready to fly away from this pond forever. Marco had his little suitcase strapped to him and his little aviator cap on. Mariposa gave him a little shot of bourbon-infused nectar and put him in the overhead, and off they flew into the night.

Now the bourbon-infused nectar helped, because Marco was afraid of heights. He had once gotten vertigo by getting up on a lily pad, and had vowed after the near fatal field trip with Mariposa never to fly again, unless he, himself turned into a butterfly, and now here he was flying, or being flown rather, on the erratic wings of Mariposa. He thought dreamily that this was the power of love, and then he threw up over the side as Mariposa took a sudden dip.

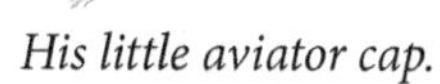

His little aviator cap.

"Turbulence," she shouted back at Marco.

Marco closed his eyes and felt sleepy from all the excitement and the alcohol and he dozed dreamily through clouds and mist. He opened one eye and saw they that were flying awfully high and still ascending. His little head throbbed inside his aviator cap, but he thought she knew what she was doing.

Then he thought, "No, she doesn't know what she is doing, but it's too late now."

He would try to sleep. He felt the warmth of Mariposa's abdomen. She told him she would sing him a lullaby. Marco shouted he would just as soon she concentrate on her flying. Marco had never heard Mariposa sing before since he was underage and unable to go to the "Chicken or Egg" pub, so he closed his eyes and waited for her mellifluous voice. Then he heard a sound like a screeching cicada. He wondered if those were the landing gears rubbing, or they had entered the air space of migrating geese, when he discovered it was Mariposa singing. It wasn't beautiful or melodious at all, it was awful. And besides that, she was singing, "Froggie went a'courtin, he did ride, uh-huh," which was the last song that poor Marco wanted to hear. How could a creature this lovely sound so bad? Maybe it was the altitude. Maybe they were breaking some sort of sound barrier, but one thing was for sure, there would have to be a change of plans. There would be no Broadway shows, and how could he break it to her that she was an awful singer.

Suddenly, there was another terrible noise above Mariposa's singing. And a bright light flashed like lightning and all of a sudden they were falling, spiraling downward in wounded circles. He could see Mariposa's wing was torn. Something had hit them, or God had struck down Mariposa for singing. He held on as they fell and fell. Was this the end for our little intrepid hero? Our slitherer and sojourner. Struck down at the very beginning of his journey. Think Marco, think! There must be something he can do. "I don't want to die. Especially if the last thing I experienced was Mariposa's singing."

Surely this can't be the end. He struggled to get a better look at their falling. He could see the ground coming up from below. They were no longer spiraling but dropping through the sky. Marco strained to do something, but what? Then suddenly, he felt something inside him, on either side, opening. He strained and felt something, though he did not know what. He could hear Mariposa crying as she held on to him.

"Good bye my little slug," she sobbed.

Then suddenly, they weren't falling any more. But they hadn't crashed and they weren't dead. Where were they? They both opened their eyes and they were hanging from some sort of string, but how?

It was Marco. Marco Tad Polo. He had managed to sprout his arms at just the right time, and in the last possible second he had reached up and grabbed the line as they passed by.

"Your arms, Marco. Your arms. You grew arms and they saved us. Your arms are now my second favorite body part of yours. It makes me want to sing," Mariposa threw back her jubilant butterfly head and gave Marco the thousand eye wink that was as seductive as a wink from the universe itself.

"No. That's okay. Don't sing. It might vibrate us loose. We'll have to figure out how to get down, and what this string is connected to…Wow! Arms. I didn't know I had arms. Now I can learn to play the guitar if we ever survive this. Here, let me give you a hug."

But Marco, who had only had arms for a minute or two, didn't realize if you let go of one thing to hold on to another thing, well, something would have to give. So suddenly they plummeted downward, but luckily the string that Marco was clinging to was attached to a grapevine, so they were close to the ground.

They landed softly in the dirt amid a long row of grapevines in a small vineyard (small to us, but very large and frightening to our two crash victims). And as they lay in a crumpled heap in the soft earth, Marco reached over and hugged Mariposa for the very first time, and they made love, and Mariposa screamed and quaked and it sounded eerily like her singing, but in this context it was beautiful.

When they had finished they lay back, exhausted, and Mariposa took out a cigarette, and gave her last one to Marco, and the sky begin to color in the pinkness of dawn.

"I wonder where we are?" Marco said as he blew smoke out into the half light.

"I don't know, Marco. Xanadu maybe?" Mariposa tried to move her torn wing.

Suddenly a dark shadow loomed over them and something spoke from the shadow.

"You are on the South Mountain. You are in a vineyard. Grapes into wine," spoke the voice.

"Who are you?" Marco asked fearfully, holding Mariposa closer, as if to protect her.

"I am the Early Bird. I catch the worm. Are you a worm with arms?"

"No. I am Marco Tad Polo, and this is my lover, Mariposa Monarcha. We have fallen from the sky. Please, please don't eat us. Or, take me if you must, but please don't eat Mariposa."

"Don't worry, my small friend. I'm not going to eat you. And the butterfly is poisonous to me. I am the early bird and you would have to get up quite early to trick me, unless you are the Night Owl. Beware the Night Owl. He is the wisest."

"Who?"

"Exactly."

"But I've learned that anything as beautiful as a butterfly is poison. To eat or drink of such beauty will seduce you and then kill you. Like a moth to a flame…Anyway, I am the Early Bird and I get the worm, and there are plenty of worms here in the vineyard. They do the dirty work and build tunnels and make the ground rich. Listen closely, be still. Can you hear them? Can you feel the vvibrations? It's the worms at work. They never stop. They are all over the world. It's global worming."

"Early Bird. We are tired and hungry. Mariposa's wing is torn and I need water. Can you help us?" Marco spoke with more confidence and less fear.

"Yes. There is a small stream just over there, within slither distance. They use it to irrigate the vineyard. There is even a patch of milkweed by the stream for the butterfly. There are many odd creatures here because of all the wine and insecticides. At least that's my theory. You might meet the Spring Chicken or the Mad Hornet, or the Mistle Toads. There's the Frog Prince, the Jitter Bugs, and the Buddha Pest. Weird, but mostly not dangerous. And all the wine you can drink."

"Wine?" Mariposa raised her head and opened her eyes for the first time through this encounter. Marco was afraid she had gone into shock from her torn wing. He was worried because if a butterfly's wing is torn, it can lead to depression and even death, and he knew Mariposa's mental state was already a little sketchy at best.

"All the wine you can drink," the Early Bird assured her.

"Is there Karaoke? Oh Marco, maybe we can stay here for a while. Maybe my wing can heal, or maybe there is a plastic sturgeon in the stream and I can get my wing repaired and a shot of Botox, too."

"Yes. We'll get you fixed up, and we can stay here. Really, we have no choice." Marco was relieved that Mariposa seemed okay, and he just secretly hoped there was no Karaoke here.

"Okay. Good luck. Perhaps I'll see you in the morning. Remember, I am the Early Bird, and I always get my worm." And with that he flew off wormward, Marco supposed, and for the time being Marco and Mariposa slept in the same dream and felt the soft vibrations of the worms at work before they made the slithering, broken—winged journey to the stream by the vineyard.

Butterfly in Repose

Mariposa, who was no juicy caterpillar anymore, whose wings, even back when they were complete, untorn, were already beginning to sag, who knew the truth about her situation—a butterfly, however beautiful, is only a temporal creature limping through its final metamorphosis—told Marco, her increasingly horny little slug (yes, he seemed to be getting accustomed to the carnal pleasures Mariposa, his wicked little English teacher, had introduced him to) that they had arrived at Xanadu, paradise, but now she wasn't so sure this was any kind of paradise at all.

They had landed on soft grass. Stalks of some sort, woody and thick, rising up all around them, but at measured intervals—evidence of human occupation, which made Mariposa nervous. Above them, against the opening blue of the sky, Mariposa spotted clusters of deep purple—fruit, she thought. Non-pondland fruit. Grapes, she suspected, but she couldn't say for sure. She'd only read of such exotic wonders.

"Xanadu, maybe." Mariposa amended, trying to move her wing. She winced—it hurt like hell—but Marco, excited by all that was happening—the near crash-landing, the passionate lovemaking (nothing like thank-god-we're-still-alive sex, with the added intimacy made possible by Marco's new, life-saving arms)—didn't notice.

She lit Marco a cigarette, her last, and taking it from his lips, she stroked his nascent mustache, straggly and cute. She took a drag. Oh, Marco, she thought. He had saved them. She had nearly killed them, but he had saved them. Beautiful, brave Marco.

Clearly, he adored her, and this saddened her. Mariposa worried that she was no good for him. She knew so much more about the big scary world, and now she'd launched him into it. She had corrupted him, and not just in the way the mothers back at the pond had feared. She had corrupted—would corrupt, she couldn't change that now—his spirit. His sweet tadpolian heart.

As they lay there, Mariposa suddenly became aware of a kind of far-off whirring, almost an insectlian buzzing, like a bee or a wasp or perhaps only a house fly. Except the droning was very small, almost unnoticeable and not noticed at all by sweet, slimy-eared Marco, and yet seemed to come from very far away. Mariposa felt the buzzing in her wings, and the edges of the tear in her wing ruffled painfully.

And then, so quickly Mariposa couldn't be certain it had happened at all, the sky flashed. The entirety of it bright-white, dazzling, for the smallest fraction of a second. A snap of light too quick to really see.

Marco seemed to notice this, or to almost notice it. He blinked up at Mariposa, a question in his eyes.

But just then, the early morning sky, brightening to blue, was once again interrupted, this time by a huge shadow falling over them. Marco quaked at her side, but Mariposa, still mystified by the dim, untraceable buzzing and the quick shot of light, was unafraid of something as pedestrian as a run-of-the-mill predator. An aging butterfly whose last hope for fame had just been dashed was too bitter and sad for conventional fear. It might end this way: being eaten alive by some unknown creature in this unknown place, her wonderful young lover at her side. But, then, would that be so bad? Surely there were worse ways to go. Her wing was broken. Her beauty, as beauty does, had reached its peak. Such is the nature of things: decline is so quickly on the heels of perfection, they seem to happen simultaneously.

But no, no. Sweet Marco. She would have to protect him somehow. Protect him in this moment, from this imminent threat. Protect him from whatever the far-off buzzing was—a machine? A great big monstrous human machine?—and from the blip of electric light, as big as the sky—and from his own hopeful heart. A young heart—too young and hopeful to even comprehend the sadness and loss this glorious and terrible world might offer.

The shadow—a bird, Mariposa saw—explained that they were in a place called South Mountain. A vineyard, he explained, though Miss Mariposa, college-educated, had already figured that much out. She was much heartened by the prospect of wine.

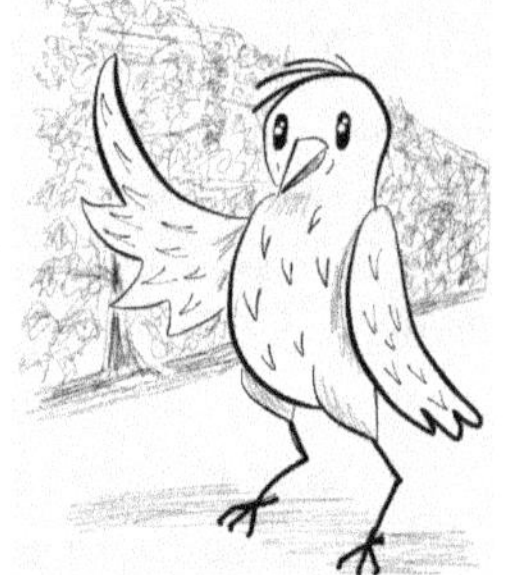

The Early Bird.

Marco was holding her close now, needlessly fearful of the bird. Though the bird towered over them and was quite huge from their perspective, Mariposa understood he was just a little brown sparrow. And, though she already knew much of what the sparrow, who called himself The Early Bird, went on to explain about the dangers of owls, whose large demon eyes shone in the night, and about the poisonous nature of butterflies, of beautiful things in general, she tried to appear to be listening. Really she was thinking of the wine and worrying over how in the hell was she going to score a new pack of cigarettes.

Finally, The Early Bird, having completed his catalog of all the disfigured, human-touched, and just plain weird denizens of the vineyard and a lengthy sermon on the glorious importance of worms, flew away and Mariposa once again ravaged young Marco—oh god, how she loved to corrupt Marco again and again…she corrupted his brains out—the two fell into the same dream while, in the earth below them, unseen and unseeing worms forged underground passage-ways and ate and ate and ate, converting dead matter into fuel for the living.

Mariposa, though dreaming contentedly cuddled up with her sweet little slug, was also in anguish, listening for the far-off buzzy grumble that had seemed to come from the ends of the earth. As she listened, she was also watching the sky, unblinking, for another quick flash of light and making her plans. She pondered: how would she set Marco free? She knew he might, once he sprouted his other set of limbs and gained jumping power, leave her anyway. This was the natural order of things: a frog with jumping legs had to travel. But, if he insisted on staying with the crippled, aging butterfly, she would have to find another way. She dreamed, sweetly, and planned, somberly, and cried her tiny, poisonous butterfly tears. Marco, exhausted from the various excitements of the past twelve hours, slept on, oblivious.

They passed the morning this way, making love and dreaming. Finally, in the early afternoon, they made their slithering, limping way to the stream where Mariposa drank deeply from the milkweed blossom while Marco frolicked in the toxic pond. As Mariposa drank, she kept one eye open, fearing the arrival of the Spring Chicken the chatty little sparrow had told them about. Thankfully, he didn't show, and while Mariposa once thought she caught a glimpse of the Frog Prince's crown and the shadowy outline of what might have been a Mistle Toad—she had to admit she was curious about that one: what would a Mistle Toad look like?—they encountered only ordinary-world pond creatures, tiny minnows and water-skaters and such. A clutch of tadpoles, inferior in every way, Mariposa believed, to her sweet Marco, and a snapping turtle, who was rather curt and rude to them, and a too-friendly dragonfly whom Mariposa wished away. She'd always found the oblong iridescent wings of a dragonfly unseemly and she thought dragonflies were as annoying as mosquitoes, if, blessedly, somewhat rarer.

The stupid creature—dragonflies have the tiniest, skitterish brains—seemingly oblivious to Mariposa's disdain, hovered, as dragonflies are wont to do.

He said, "It's not very often we encounter anyone from the outside. Tell me, what is the world like?"

Marco hesitated, then began, "Well, the pond we come from is full of dancing June Bugs and madly quacking ducks and terrible spiders who try to eat everyone."

Mariposa sighed. "And karaoke." To demonstrate how much she longed for her beloved karaoke bar, she threw back her little butterfly head and sang. "And I will always love you…" She sighed again and tried to ignore what she was certain she saw: her sweet slimy slug flinching at her singing. The dragonfly shuttered, noticeably disturbed. But Mariposa continued, explaining, "I was going for the Dolly version, rather than Whitney. Not much of a Whitney fan."

And, then, when the two remained silent, "Oh, how I miss the Chicken and Egg Pub! I never should have left. Oh, Broadway. Broadway. Tell me, dragonfly"—the dragonfly had told them his name but Mariposa hadn't bothered to remember it—"where is this wine The Early Bird spoke of?"

The dragonfly finally proved to be of service and led them over through a flower garden—lovely, but frightening too, to find yet more proof of human occupation—and across a small field to a swampy red puddle of squashed grapes, fermented in the warmth of the sun.

"Merlot," the dragonfly explained.

"I don't care." Mariposa answered, kneeling at the side of the puddle to drink.

And finally the dragonfly, laughing to himself—he'd never seen a drunk butterfly—winged away.

Later, Mariposa, drunk and happy, lounging by the wine puddle, remarked to Marco about the lack of deformed pond creatures. "Maybe," she said, "it was the Early Bird whose brain was scrambled by the insecticides and the wine." It was early evening now, the sky deepening into a plumy smoke color, and they were drowsing by the stream. "I was hoping to find a plastic sturgeon, or at least the Buddha Pest. I could use some religion now." Mariposa sniffled. "Or at least a little prayer. Or, fuck it all, just a damn cigarette!"

Marco, his tiny mustache twitching, reached for Mariposa. He embraced her hard, ungiving body with his new arms, holding her tight against his slimy softness.

Pulling back, he kissed her, then whispered, "I have a surprise for you."

At first, Mariposa couldn't guess what the object Marco pulled from the weeds behind him was. It wasn't until Marco settled the bundle of broken reeds and bits of pond grass unto his lap and began to pluck at its strings that Mariposa understood.

"Oh, Marco! A guitar! How did you…"

But he was plucking and listening and making small adjustments. Mariposa watched his face rather than his hands as he worked. He squinted his eyes and wrinkled his brow and nodded a little to himself, and then his little guitar produced a sound he liked, and everything settled on his sweet, green, newly and thinly mustached face. He closed his eyes, strummed his guitar, and opened his mouth to sing.

Mariposa closed her eyes, too, and let the tadpole's little song—he had only learned how to play today—carry her away. It was a song about a butterfly with angels in her hair. This made no sense, and it probably wasn't really what Marco was singing; Mariposa was so drunk now, she hardly remembered her own name. And besides that, Mariposa had an odd imagination and old ears. And besides that, she liked the image: a broken butterfly with angels entwined in her antennae—even she couldn't imagine herself with hair. She saw herself flying away, not on the lift of her own old wings, but lifted by tiny twinkling angels.

"Into the deepest blue sky," she told Marco when he'd finished playing. But it was quickly growing dark now, and Mariposa waited impatiently for Marco to lay his guitar down so she could climb on top of him. She kissed him and wrapped her legs around him and nearly swallowed him whole in her passion. My god, she whispered. It was like the prayer she had hoped for earlier, but better. The stars blinked on, one by one, in the sky above them and Mariposa screamed out, her ecstasy piercing the darkness and the quiet. She came again and again, and the sounds of their lovemaking moved over the surface of the pond, rippling ever so slightly in the wind.

But then, after her screams had dwindled to whimpers and finally given over to soft, contented sighs, the buzzing of unknown origin droned down on them from the sky again. It was, as it had been earlier in the day, almost too quiet to hear. But this time it was a sustained metallic-ish hum, then a strengthening whirring until it finally very nearly clanged. It filled Mariposa's tiny butterfly ears and overwhelmed her and shook poor little Marco's jellyish body until he panted with queasiness. They held on to each other in their fright, and simultaneously searched the now-black sky: what was it? And where was it coming from?

Mariposa wondered, with paralyzing alarm: what creature or man-made beast was capable of producing such a noise?

She thought, it's death, come for me. Of course, it made sense to Mariposa, who, like most butterflies, was an extremely vain and self-centered creature: death, when it came for her, would fill the sky with its terribleness, its darkness.

And then, just as suddenly, the booming clamor seemed to shift, as if it were a physical being with a physical body, adjusting itself, and then dissipated, shimmering away into the darkness.

Later, after Mariposa had whispered soothing noises into Marco's ears and finally managed to get him to sleep, she herself had trouble sleeping. She had intended to leave Marco early in the morning, to set out hitchhiking her way back home to the old pond, the home she and Marco had left behind just two days earlier in hopes of a better, more exciting life in New York City. She would leave Marco here, in the vineyard, a place that wasn't terribly exciting but at least wasn't home, either. During their lovemaking, she had moved her spindly black butterfly arms down the length of his slick tadpole body and discovered two more lumps, barely even there yet, below his arms. His jumping legs were emerging. And now, as she stood over him, bending to kiss his cheek, she saw the whole of him shining in the starlight: his tail had grown smaller just since this morning.

Oh, it was happening. Marco Tad Polo moving along in his life, maturing much too quickly. She wouldn't wait until morning. She was awake now, and sad, and everything was changing. Her wing throbbed with pain and drooped miserably at her side. It was a growing weight, this broken wing of hers, and she walked lopsided, torturously. Mariposa hobbled.

And then, she knew. She knew. She wouldn't be going home.

She drew close to the puddle of Merlot. How fitting, that this should happen here: she was going to literally drown her sorrows in wine. Too vinegary, but it would do. It would be fine. Everything would be just fine now.

She closed her eyes, stepped into the puddle, clenching stones in her tiny butterfly hands since butterflies don't wear coats with pockets. The wine felt as warm as bathwater. It embraced her.

But then, there came again the flash of light filling up the sky, but this time it didn't stop, but flashed again and again, like a strobe light at a nightclub or the flicker of a million camera bulbs popping at once. And with the lights, there came the buzzing, larger this time, throbbing hugely across the sky.

She didn't hear Marco calling for her, nor did she hear him slither into the pond from behind her. But she felt his little tadpolian arm on her back and the two of them held onto each other as they slowly turned their heads to look into the sky.

Marco Saves the Day at Night

Marco reclined on the leaf, and with another leaf, tried to cover Mariposa from the night chill. He then looked up at the stars and wondered how many orgasms Mariposa had just had since he could only count to ten, and at ten Mariposa was just getting warmed up.

Poor Marco was beginning to understand the complexity of being in love with a complicated creature like Mariposa. He should be dating an amoeba or something. And now he had to worry about Mariposa's torn wing, her subsequent depression, and her insatiable appetite. The pond of merlot would help, but he would have to find some cigarettes for her soon, or she would drive him crazy.

If that wasn't enough, he had to worry about his own maturation and how to stop it. It felt like his poor brain was growing arms and legs and trying to jump out of his little tadpole head. He ran his new fingers along his new mustache, and felt the bumps of legs beneath his skin which was turning rather translucent. That wasn't an attractive look either. Maybe he wasn't going to turn into a frog at all. Maybe he would just disappear. His tail was growing shorter and he was pretty sure something else was growing shorter too since he and Mariposa had made love almost constantly since they had left. He knew once his legs came in he would have to try and stop the process.

Marco, being a tadpole of action, shook off his rather worrisome reverie. He kissed Mariposa gently on the cheek. She snored softly—a gentle, musical, butterfly snore. Marco slithered off as Mariposa slept fitfully beneath the cover of the leaf, her torn wing twitching.

"This was a Vineyard, right? So there had to be a lot of creatures and towns and places nearby, and cigarettes and good drugs." Marco felt perhaps he could find an apothecary. There must be some concoction or potion that could halt the maturation process. He was Marco Tad Polo, not Marco Von Frog, and he was determined to stay Marco Tad Polo. He saw himself with his arms and legs and small, but shapely tail as a type of Satyr, a mythical creature, half beast and half… half what?

Marco snapped himself out of his fantasy. "Focus, Marco, focus." He realized he was somehow adopting Mariposa's mood swings, and he didn't need that. Right now he was a scared tadpole slithering through the grass looking for a bar or a place that sold cigarettes. Before long, Marco heard something like music coming from somewhere just off the vineyard row. He came to something that looked like an alley and followed the sound of the music. It was a type of music he had never heard before. Suddenly, the alley opened up into a larger street and he saw a terrifying sight. A creature that looked like a giant tadpole lying in front of him. The creature was wearing large sunglasses and was playing a mouth harp and singing. Marco approached cautiously and stopped and began to snap his fingers and tap his invisible foot inside his skin.

"Hey, man, that's cool," Marco heard himself say. He was trying to be cool, but he was very scared. His knees were knocking on the inside and that made his little belly shake like jelly. He made himself continue, "I'm a stranger here and I was wandering and wondering if you could tell me if there was a club, or a bar, or a store nearby—and an apothecary or doctor."

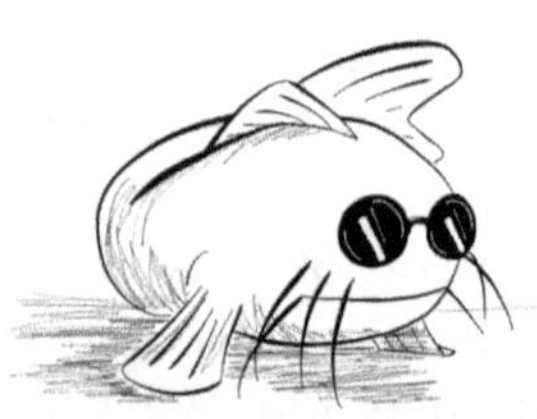

Blind Catfish Walkin'

The creature looked at Marco with his right blind eye. "Where did you come from? Did you just drop out of the sky?"

"Huh, yes, actually, I did. I was riding this butterfly that I'm in love with and there was some sort of solar flair or something and it zapped us because we were flying to New York, wherever that is, so Mariposa, that's the butterfly, could make it on Broadway, but then we fell out of the sky…"

Marco paused breathlessly. The creature looked at Marco with his left blind eye and spoke in a deep, resonant voice, "Man, I've got to stop dropping so much acid. My hallucinations are starting to talk back to me." He then begin to sing:

Oh, I'm a catfish who can't go into the water now.
Oh I'm just a catfish who can't go into the water now.
I'm just a walking catfish who is afraid he might drown.

The catfish then wailed on his mouth harp and Marco's life changed forever. It was the first time that Marco heard the blues.

Marco spoke. "Man, that was amazing. I'm a tadpole, and I have my arms and I want to learn to play the guitar, but I don't want to turn into a frog. I want to stay a tadpole or actually somewhere in between a tad toad or a frogpolian because I'm in love with a butterfly who has a torn wing and I'm afraid she won't love me if I turn into a disgusting frog."

The Catfish blew a flatted seventh note and began to sing:

I woke up this morning I had the frog legs blues.
Yeah, I woke up this morning and I had the frog legs blues.
I want to stay a tadpole, my baby wants me to stay a tadpole too.

My baby she likes to climb my tadpole.

Yeah, my baby likes to climb my tadpole.

If you go down to the crossroads, maybe the devil will freeze your soul.

The catfish looked at Marco with his right blind eye. "Well, little Tad Toad, I tell you what I'm going to do. I need a guitar player. A long time ago, a well-meaning hooker worm gave me a guitar, but seeing that I don't have any arms it wasn't much good to me. If you go down the tunnel here a-ways, it's leaning up against my catfish couch under the Dung Beetles Blues Band poster. Bring it out and I'll show you a few chords."

Marco quickly slithered down the tunnel that opened up into a small room. The room was lit dimly by a lava lamp and he saw the guitar leaning against the couch. He picked it up and held it in his new hands and knew he had found a part of his destiny.

The catfish taught him a few chords, but Marco knew he had to get back to Mariposa soon before she woke up and freaked out. The catfish looked at Marco with his left blind eye.

"Go ahead and take it with you. Come back tomorrow and we'll jam."

"Yeah, we'll jam," replied Marco wondering what he meant by "jam."

"And there's the Xanadu club just down the alley. It's a jazz club." Catfish winked with his right blind eye.

"Cool," said Marco. He didn't know what jazz was either. "You can find various apothecaries in Xanadu, if you get my drift."

"Yeah, daddio," Marco didn't really get the drift, but he was trying. He then remembered that if he could score some cigarettes, things would go much better when he got back to Mariposa.

"Excuse me," stammered Marco, "What is your name?"

"They call me 'Blind Catfish Walkin.'"

"Huh, Mr. Blind Catfish Walkin, can you tell me where I can get some cigarettes, for my main squeeze, you know." (Marco was practicing talking like a bluesman.) "She's a butterfly. Very high strung. Very flighty."

"A tadpole in love with a butterfly? That's a blues song if I've ever heard one. You're going to need more than cigarettes. But yeah, I've got a carton of Lucky Strokes inside the tunnel there, on the table by the couch, next to the bong. Take'em. You'll owe me a couple gigs though. Practice that guitar. Learn the blues."

"I will, Mr. Blind Catfish Walkin." Marco grabbed the guitar and cigarettes and slithered off as fast as he could. His greenish glow now had a slight blue tint to it or so he imagined.

When he returned, Mariposa was still sleeping. Her broken wing twitching rhythmically. Marco hid the guitar and cigarettes in the grass and squeezed in beside her as the day was beginning to fade. He held her gently and she stirred slightly as if rising to the rim of her dream and then sinking back into it. He inhaled her breathing and blew it back out into invisible smoke rings like angel dragons. He thanked the little cosmos for his arms and fingers and for this quiet moment where the heart of love dwelled. He loved Mariposa so deeply and in loving so deeply he feared losing her. He feared his coming legs. He feared the passage of time. He feared the change toward frog hood. Amphibalescence. He feared Mariposa would stop loving him, and that one day soon she would be drunk and just fly off with some studly butterfly. Marco feared fear and the fear of all that was fearful. And then he had an epiphany. This was the blues. He had the blues, but he was the blues and when the blues meet the blues, then the blues never leaves. He was a blues man, actually he was amphibian, and he knew to sing the blues away was to sing the fear way. To look the stupid fear in the face. Make the fear get that grasshopper-in-the-headlights look on its face. To freeze it with the Houdini-one-shot. To realize that in this moment he loved Mariposa with all his heart and he felt and held the moment as tightly as he held Mariposa, and part of the Blues was knowing how sweet that love is, and that somewhere it has to end, and somewhere Mariposa would be waking up.

Then, Mariposa opened a thousand eyes sleepily.

"I have a surprise for you." Marco slithered a short distance into the grass and returned with his guitar.

"Oh Marco—a guitar! How did you…"

Marco tuned the guitar as best he could, and for the first time Marco played the Blues: Tadpole loved the butterfly. She had angels in her hair.

"Oh yeah, Tadpole loved the butterfly. She had angels in her hair.

And when they made love, there were angels everywhere."

"Oh Marco," and before Marco was finished playing the turnaround, Mariposa was on top of him. He set the guitar down as gently as he could upon the grass, and Mariposa kissed him hard. It turned out Mariposa loved the blues. Ninety-six butterfly orgasms later, she had reduced Marco to a puddle of tadpole, a churning urn of burning fungus, a demolition derby hunk of steaming slug, a napalm bomb that had just blown his little mind, a hunk-a-hunk of burning love.

Marco was almost afraid to give Mariposa a cigarette. He was afraid she would be so grateful she would jump on him again, and he wasn't sure he could take it. He looked down at his tadpole penis. It was more "tad," than "pole" and one more round with Mariposa and he was afraid it might retreat like a frightened turtle. But now he wanted a cigarette as much as Mariposa, so he rolled over and took a long drink from the pond of Merlot, and that revived him a bit. He slithered into the long grass and came back with the cigarettes. Mariposa kissed him over and over but Marco with his now nimble fingers stuck a cigarette into Mariposa's mouth and lit it with a match. Marco lit his cigarette off the same match and they lay back and stared into the blackness.

Then Marco heard it…At first, he thought it was just his head buzzing from all of the love making, but then it got louder and louder. Perhaps it was Mariposa, sometimes she got a bit buzzy, but no, it was coming from somewhere above them. It got louder and buzzier. It sounded like it was getting nearer and nearer. It seemed to vibrate the air around them. Marco held on to Mariposa tightly. Where was it coming from? What could it be?

"Let's put it over here." A human voice, a young female human voice, deafening and abrasive. Marco pulled Mariposa into a clump of grass, and they cowered there together.

"No, no, over here. We can hang it from this tree limb. Here I'm going to light it up," shouted a young male voice. "Dad said to put the bug zapper as close to the middle of the vineyard as we could."

Marco could see the huge feet and leg trunks of the two humans. He was practically invisible but Mariposa with her bright orange wings was surely visible beside the tree trunk. He tried to cover her wings with his brownish, greenish, now slightly bluish dull color, but he couldn't cover all of her. Suddenly, not only was there the loud buzzing, but now a bright, blinding light shining just above them. Out of nowhere came a group of young mayflies. They surrounded Marco and Mariposa, squealing and shouting playfully.

"Hey, watch this," and one of them shot up and flew directly into the bright buzzing light. There was a sickly, sizzling sound and the mayfly simply disappeared, sizzled out of existence, incinerated by the heat of the bug zapper.

A second mayfly jumped up. "Watch this," it screamed and he shot up and flew directly into the bright light, just as his companion had done with the same sizzling result. This was repeated many times until there was only one mayfly remaining.

Marco spoke to the last one in a whisper, "This doesn't seem to be such a good idea."

The mayfly looked at Marco blankly and squealed, "Watch this. It's Broadway."

And that was the end of that.

The human voices laughed as they watched a variety of insects fly into the irresistible lure of the bright light only to go down, or up, in flames.

"Look. A butterfly on the ground. There." Then the monstrous hand of the male reached down and pulled Mariposa out of the arms of Marco Tad Polo. He tried to hold on to her, but then he was afraid he might injure her further. Maybe the human would just look at her and let her go.

"Here, give it to me," squealed the female human monster. "Look! Its wing is torn. Let me see it."

The young male monster held Mariposa by the legs and then he held her very close to the the bug zapper. Mercifully, Marco could not see what was going on but could only hear the confusion of voices.

"Don't, don't burn it up! Give it to me!"

The male human monster held Mariposa so close to the heat of the zapper that he could hear her wings start to sizzle in the heat.

"No, no, stop it!" yelled the female monster.

She grabbed the boy's wrist and dug her nails into his skin until he dropped the butterfly. Mariposa fell back into the grass a few feet from where Marco hid. The boy chased the girl and they disappeared with their horrible monster voices into the darkness.

When they had gone, and only the buzzing and the terrible light remained, Marco slithered to Mariposa. She was unconscious and unresponsive. Was she alive or dead? She was lying on her back, her beautiful wings singed by the heat. She looked like a ghost of herself, or her own guardian angel. But now brave Marco had to be her real guardian angel. He held her and rocked her and cried tadpole tears that had little arms and legs inside them, and sang her his blues song about how she had angels in her hair, but it was no use. There was only one hope. He had to drag Mariposa's lifeless body to the pond of Merlot.

As he started to drag her, he noticed that all the fine hairs from her body had been singed away, and she seemed blonder and paler and appeared to be "almost what an angel would look like," Marco thought. But he had to focus. Mariposa seemed to be breathing ever so shallowly, so she was still alive and Marco had to save her. He would have to muster all his strength to make it to the pond that was at least a meter away. As he tried to grasp her by the legs so he wouldn't hurt her, he noticed that her torn wing was no longer torn, but seemingly fused and welded back together by the great heat of the light. At least that was something. A good omen perhaps.

And so it took to the first light of morning for Marco to slowly drag the lifeless Mariposa to the side of the pond. The brown, green, glowing with a slight blue tint tadpole hero and his beautiful, orange, slightly blonder love moving almost imperceptibly along the grass toward the pond of wine.

When they finally reached the pond, the sun was climbing in the sky. Marco didn't know if Mariposa was dead or alive, but he used his little aviator cap as a cup to dip the dark wine red liquid and he held it to Mariposa's lips. Still unconscious, she could not drink, so Marco rubbed the Merlot on her lips, and then he rubbed the wine all over her body, soothing the places that were still warm with the heat of the killing light. The Merlot spilled onto the ground, and the grass and the kind earth drank of the wine, and the Vineyard, like the moss and the algae, had a soul and was alive and it took pity on our kind hero and heroine, and the ground began to vibrate gently beneath them. It massaged Marco's small tired body, and it massaged the lifeless body of our beautiful Mariposa. Marco knew it was global worming, and as he held Mariposa, he drank of the wine until he was quite tipsy, and he looked down at Mariposa and suddenly she opened her butterfly eyes and blinked, and Marco cried and thanked the vineyard for helping him save Mariposa.

Mariposa's eyes were wide open but they seemed not to see. They stared blankly up at Marco like she was a newborn caterpillar. She moved unsteadily and sat up beside Marco and finally spoke.

"Who are you?"

"I'm Marco Tad Polo," Marco said, rather confused by the question. "We flew here together. We are in love."

"We are? Where are we?" Mariposa looked confused and frightened. She sat up slowly and looked around. She looked at Marco as if he were Frankenstein and she the bride waking. Her antennae were erect. She recoiled from Marco.

"We are in a friendly vineyard. You've just been in a terrible accident. You were nearly burned up. I had to save you." Marco answered but wondered desperately why Mariposa was asking these questions.

"An accident? I was? I don't remember anything. I can't remember anything. Who am I?!" This time Mariposa seemed to relax a little. She again took in her surroundings—looked down at her newly repaired but paler wings.

Marco stared at the lovely angelic Mariposa and he thought hard. Apparently, Mariposa had some sort of insect amnesia, either from the traumatic experience of the death light or she struck her head when she fell back to the earth, but she didn't know who she was. Marco thought hard. He loved Mariposa with all his heart and he wanted to save her and perhaps that meant saving her from herself. He loved her but he always wished that she was happier, less neurotic. Perhaps here was an opportunity.

"Who am I? What's my name?" Mariposa pleaded.

Marco decided. "Your name is Marilyn Merlot. You are a beautiful monarch butterfly and you love to diagram sentences in the clouds. You make love insatiably (he didn't want to change everything), and you have a lovely singing voice. I am Marco Tad Polo. I'm your guitar player and lover. And it's my birthday too. Would you sing happy birthday to me, Marilyn Merlot?"

Mariposa, now Marilyn Merlot, stood up and smiled seductively, and sang in an amazingly husky, sexy voice, "Happy birthday, to you. Happy birthday to you Happy birthday, Mr. President."

"That's Marco." Piped up Marco.

"Happy birthday, Marco. Happy birthday to you." And she kissed Marco passionately.

"Would you like a glass of Merlot, Marilyn?" Marco asked.

Butterfly Heaven

It had been a horrifying ordeal. To cower below with a suddenly and inexplicably blue-tinged Marco in the grass while, above them, a tiny legion of mayflies, every one of them dumber than the last, was zapped by the bug zapper. The last one yelled, "Watch this, it's Broadway!" and Mariposa, infuriated with the creature's stupidity and with such blasphemy—besmirching Broadway's good name, even out of gleeful ignorance was, in Mariposa's book, a heinous crime—thought, "Die! Die! You stupid son of a bitch!" And then, happily—zap!—the little fucker was incinerated.

"Look," came the voice of a child. "A butterfly on the ground. There."

Now descended the wretched, grimy hand of a human. It was larger than the sky and as pale and fungisy as a mushroom. Mariposa gripped Marco tighter as the hand drew nearer, but it was no use. Of course, the hand would want her. Humans have a history for plucking butterflies from the insides of flowers, from their resting places, and, at this minute, from the arms of their inexhaustible young lovers. Yes, even in a moment like this—human hand falling from the sky and, now, closing its monster-human fingers to pinch her wing—Mariposa was falling into a passionate swoon, her desire for Marco, who was both virile and sweet—a damn sexy combination—was made all the stronger for the straits they were in. As Mariposa was wrenched from Marco's arms and lifted thousands of insect-miles into the air, she couldn't help but wish she could have just five more minutes with her young lover. If thank-god-we're-still-alive sex is pretty hot, oh-god-we're-about-to-die sex is downright electrifying.

But, alas, this was not to be. Mariposa and Marco would not get a last quickie. The end had come too suddenly. Mariposa closed her eyes.

"Here, give it to me," the gruesome human girl said. "Look! Its wing is torn! Let me see it."

Mariposa was passed from human wretchedness to human wretchedness. It was terrifying, absolutely, but more than that, it was humiliating. The hand smelled as mildew-sickly as it looked, and vaguely acrid, like the hot, singed smell of their bug zappers.

Mariposa, too exhausted and scared to even tremble, wished Marco had not saved her from her wine-slushed drowning.

The horrible hand held her close to the zapper, its light searing and awful. The heat shot through her wings, wretchedly painful, and Mariposa cried out.

Even through her closed eyelids, the light scorched her thousand butterfly eyes.

"No, no, stop it!"

But the words, human words, were so distant, Mariposa could not be sure if she heard them for real or not. She felt her body drifting, but she could not tell if she were moving upward, ascending to the sky and all that was eternal and beautiful and blue, or drifting, like a feather on the wind, slowly, peacefully, to the earth. Mariposa only knew she was moving through the sky and that the

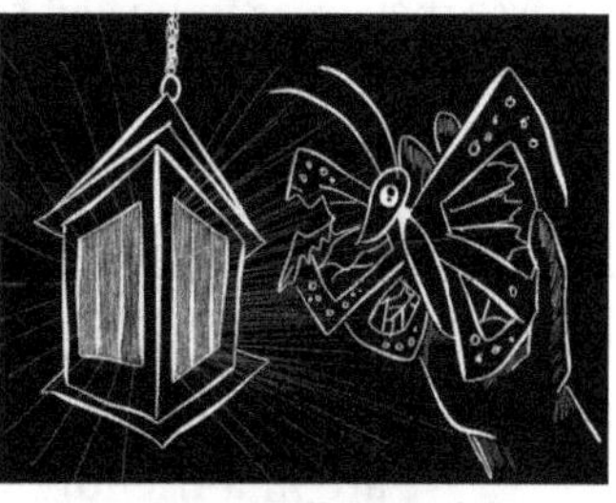

wretchedly painful

sky, though blue, was not the normal blue of a normal sky. It was liquid blue, but gauzier, and warm. Purply at the edges. If a color and that color's feeling—its softness against her new-singed body, against her resealed wing—could intoxicate a butterfly, this was that color. Everything, including the places deepest inside her, fuzzed. Even the outside world, so very far, far away, fuzzed familiarly, as if Mariposa were in thrilling, intimate contact with a star, with a thousand stars, with the farthest ones—the ones unseeable from the planet Earth.

She floated here, in this dreamy blue world, and breathed in peace, peace as she'd never known it, and felt, for the first time in her life, complete.

Was she dead? She didn't know. She didn't care. She simply was. And existence, in and of itself, was enough for her now, in this moment. Every moment complete and perfect in this new, floating sphere of being.

Curiously, even though Marco wasn't there with her, or, at least not physically there with her, she felt closer to him, to the real Marco, the Marco who had sung his heart to her, who had, all the way back in the by-the-pond school, pretended to love cloud-diagramming, the Marco of huge heart and ambition and such feeling. Maybe his new blueness had something to do with the blueness she felt all around her. Maybe their love was even bigger, truer than she had once believed. Maybe love itself was bigger, truer than she had once believed.

Now, there were Marco's hands on her body, her lips. His sweet slimy tadpolian fingers finding the meeting places, body segment to body segment, of her exoskeleton. His light touch, something warm and liquid, on her legs.

Was this real? Or was it a new and altogether more pleasant feature to this new, blue, otherworldly realm of existence?

And so, when she asked him, "Who are you?" she was not asking literally who he was because of course she recognized her Marco—her dear sweet Marco—but she was still caught up in the fuzzy blue, and here, now, Marco, leaning over her, looking bluer than ever. Who was he, really? This beautiful tadpole-turning-to-frog. This amazing, amazing creature.

"I'm Marco Tad Polo," Marco said. Poor, sweet Marco. Obviously, her question had rattled him. "We flew here together. We are in love."

"We are?" Mariposa asked, unable to keep the sarcasm from her voice. Of course they were in love; it seemed beyond stupid that he had to say so, especially in light of all that Mariposa had seen, had felt in her blue daze. But the tadpole didn't seem to understand. He was still looking at her as if she frightened him. "Where are we?" Mariposa asked, though it was finally dawning on her. Where were they? Reality. Fucking human-infiltrated, non-Broadway reality. They had been such fools to believe they could escape it. Mariposa was an experienced butterfly; she should have known better.

"We are in a friendly vineyard. You've just been in a terrible accident. You were nearly burned up. I had to save you."

Oh, sweet Marco. How had he saved her? He had plucked from the most beautiful world of floating and warmth. He had saved her?

And, he had been there. In the other realm. With her. He had been there and hadn't even known it.

"Who am I?" Mariposa demanded. Of course, she knew who she was, but she wanted to see what Marco would say. Maybe it was cruel, but she couldn't resist it: she was testing him. Who was she? Did he even know who she was deep inside? He claimed to love her, and she believed he really believed he did, but, oh, he was so young. Did Marco Tad Polo, young and green and now a little blue, even really know what love was?

"Where are we?" Mariposa longed for her blue heaven. She wanted to bring Marco there, wanted to live there—abide there, forever—with him.

But the stupid little tadpole said nothing. He was squinting at her, thinking.

"Who am I?" she asked again. "What's my name?"

Oh, what hell love was. Marco hesitated, and Mariposa thought: oh, I shall smother the stupid slimy thing. He didn't even know her fucking name.

Mariposa longed to return to the beautiful warm blue ofnot-knowing.

And just as she was about to kiss him, if nothing else to free them both of this embarrassing and agonizing moment, he answered her.

"Your name is Marilyn Merlot. You are a beautiful Monarch butterfly and you love to diagram sentences in the clouds. You make love insatiably, and you have a lovely singing voice. And I am Marco Tad Polo. I'm your guitar player and lover. And it's my birthday, too. Would you sing happy birthday to me, Marilyn Merlot?"

Mariposa gasped. Her tiny butterfly heart inside her tiny hard black butterfly body contracted painfully. She thought it would stop. She wanted it to.

How could her sweet Marco, who had always adored her, who loved her, call her by a different name? Why would he want her to be somebody else? Didn't he love her as she truly was?

Goddamnit, she thought. Every man wants a bimbo. Even a slimy sweet adolescent tadpole. Even this tadpole, Marco, with his poet's heart.

But she rose up, trembling a little, and smiled the most seductive smile she could muster. It was his birthday, was it? She knew just what he wanted. But she loved this tadpole, and she would do what she had to do to make him love her back.

And so she began to sing, using a sexy husky voice that wasn't hers at all.

"Happy birthday to you. Happy birthday to you. Happy birthday, Mr. President..."

Here the miserable little pisser, who had just broken her heart into a million tiny pieces, interrupted her.

"That's Marco."

Sure, he couldn't bring himself to say her name, but insisted she use his name in this ridiculous charade. Stupid fucking male fantasy.

But, she would do it. It was him, Marco. She would do anything for him. Even this.

"Happy birthday, Marco. Happy birthday to you."

And she kissed him passionately. Her song might have been a fake, and certainly her bimbo-husky voice was. But this, this was real—Mariposa kissing Marco, the tadpole she loved.

"Would you like a glass of Merlot, Marilyn?" Marco asked, pulling away from her. He stroked the side of her face so tenderly, Mariposa could almost believe it was real. That he really loved her.

She kissed him again, a long, sad kiss. "Why, yes, Marco. A glass of Merlot would be lovely." She giggled her best bimbo giggle.

And so they lived. Days they lounged together by the insecticide-riddled pond, nights by the Merlot pond, taking frequent boozy dips. They lived and they loved, these two, though they were hardly the same tadpole and butterfly who had once upon a time dropped from the midnight sky, struck down by a magnetic solar wind.

Mariposa became so thoroughly Marilyn, husky-voiced and sexy-acting, she sometimes forgot she was pretending. The worst part was having to sound all breathless and confused. She grew impatient with herself, the way she talked, with so many breathless pauses. But it wasn't all bad, being Marilyn. It was actually at times kind of fun, playing sexy and dumb. Walking around with her upper thorax pushed out provocatively, all that male attention from the whole and unwhole insects, the ones touched by insecticides and other human atrocities. Mariposa/Marilyn wasn't the only one singed blonde by the bug zapper. There was a horsefly blanched almost completely colorless on one side, charred black on the other. His name was Ed. Ed, the whistling horsefly, a cat-calling devil if Mariposa/Marilyn ever knew one.

But Ed and the rest were no substitute for her sweet Marco, and sweet Marco, bluer, cooler, and curiously more tadpole-like than ever before. It seemed his back legs had dwindled a bit, and for a while, Mariposa/Marilyn had worried that a certain other appendage might similarly diminish. She was relieved to find this wasn't the case. Happily, this wasn't the case at all.

"Oh, Marco," her faux bimbo-self murmured. The two were lying together, tired and happy after a particularly raucous roll in the hay—or, rather, a roll in the merlot-soaked pond grass. They were sharing a cigarette. Marco always brought her cigarettes now; she knew not from where. "My holy fucking god, Marco."

"Cool, daddio," Marco said. It was something he said all the time now. Even, well, now. "Catch my drift?" he said when there was no drift to be caught. "All right," he said, coolly, nodding. "That there is the real deal," he said about everything.

Mariposa/Marilyn blew a long thin gray ribbon of smoke into the air and sighed.

"That'll do," she said, the real Mariposa slipping through for just a moment. When Marco's brow wrinkled, she added, "Daddio," in her breathless Marilyn way. "That'll do me just perfect, Daddio," she said.

But it wasn't just an annoying as hell obsession with a new set of lingo. Marco was down at the blues club, learning from some blobby gross fat blind catfish every day and he played there in some band several times a week. Mariposa was not a fan of the looped-out way this cat said the word apothecary or of the hold he seemed to have over her Marco.

Mariposa/Marilyn found the blues-talk tiresome and sometimes she was jealous of the time his music demanded of him, but, oh, when she watched him play. He closed his little tadpole eyes, lifted his little tadpole face to the sky, and, as he strummed his guitar, sang so beautifully, so soulfully, so passionately, it nearly brought tears to Mariposa/Marilyn's eyes. Marco had found his thing, his calling, his art. And it was truly a beautiful thing to behold.

So, Mariposa kept up the Marilyn charade, and, after kissing Marco good-bye each afternoon, him heading off to the club, she tried to find her own thing. Her own calling, her art. She began with dance lessons with the jitterbugs. Every afternoon, for a time, she dutifully packed a gym bag with various kinds of dance shoes—tap, clogging shoes (these were hillbilly jitterbugs), and even fucking ballet slippers. She shimmied, shook, tapped, lurched, pirouetted, and shagged.

At night, Marco's eyes shining with the joy he'd found, in his music, in his love for the bimbified Marilyn/Mariposa, shining with Merlot, he asked her, "Are you happy, my love?"

"Yes, very," she said, but later, while Marco dozed, snoring softly, Marilyn lay on her back, sucking wine from the pond beside her through a reed, and cried. Fat, poisonous butterfly tears slid down her face and seeped into the all-knowing earth.

"Marco, baby," she added, snuggling up to him. She twirled her finger around on his tadpolian chest, then lay her head on his shoulder. "Marco, honey," she purred. But she could barely stand herself. Marilyn-fucking-Merlot. Happy?

How could she possibly be happy?

The next day, she went to the Buddhapest to learn how to meditate and pray. He taught her how to center herself, speaking of lessening desire and following the eight-fold path.

And again, that night, Marco, so happy in his blues, in his music, his guitar, his blind catfish, the universe of bright stars above them, asked again, "Are you happy, Marilyn, my love?"

She was thinking she might as well give up and spend her days drinking with Ed. Maybe that was her calling: she was meant to be a drunk, drinking and drinking with a sloppy old horsefly.

But again, now, lying in the dark with her sweet Marco, whom she loved more than ever, watching him grow as a musician, Marco, becoming the tadpole he was meant to be, she answered that she was. But the tears escaped early tonight, and she was unable to stop them, and Marco, seeing her sadness, reached for her hand in the dark.

"I have a confession to make, Marilyn." He sighed, morosely, and Mariposa squeezed his squishy little tadpole hand.

"Don't," she said. Whatever it was, she simply did not want to know.

But he continued. "I think I've made a terrible mistake."

God, Mariposa thought, he sounds so old. So world-weary. So disillusioned. She couldn't let him continue this way, so she tried her usual method of quieting the young tadpole: she climbed on top of him and kissed him. She kissed him hard, so he couldn't speak, and then, she reached for his sweet little tadpolian pole, wrapping her butterfly fingers around it. She only wanted to make him forget that he wanted to say anything at all.

But Marco surprised her by turning his face away from her kisses. He put his hand on top of her hand, still lingering on his tadpole shaft, stopping her.

"Mariposa, I mean, Marilyn. I have to tell you something." He looked so determined, so serious. Mariposa released him, but remained on top of him, straddling him. She looked down at him, touched his sweet slimy slug face with her delicate butterfly fingers.

"Oh, Marco," she began, but before she could continue, she saw that Marco's attention was suddenly elsewhere. He was looking over her shoulder at something behind her, something in the ink black sky.

"Oh," he said, enraptured. "Oh, oh," he said again, and Mariposa waited for him to say something about the sky being far out or the real deal or whatever the fuck a plucky blues playing amphibian might say by way of describing a starry night, but he said, "Oh," once again and then seemed to be struck silent. Mariposa turned to see what Marco was seeing.

She feared it might be the bug zapper again, or another mother-fucking human child, but it was none of those things.

"Oh," Mariposa said. "Oooh."

It was the fuzzy blue of Mariposa's unconsciousness, her blue heaven, in a glittery, purple-edged cloud. The blue was dense and unnatural. Mariposa thought, it looks like a floating pool of spilled paint. She thought, it looks like cotton candy. It was alive; she thought there might be a million soft blue thunderbolts zinging inside it. It shimmered hugely against the black, and Mariposa could only think one thing.

"Fly me into that," Marco said.

"My thoughts exactly," she answered, sliding her body off his. She poised herself for take-off.

Neither of them thought for a second that it was too good to be true, or even wondered what it really was. Anywhere but here, Mariposa/Marilyn was thinking and not thinking. I can't fucking stand to be Marilyn Merlot for one more fucking second, she thought and she didn't think.

Only this: that beautiful blue. That otherworldly glimmering blue elongating itself, rolling open like a great cloud against the endless sky.

Still, deep, deep beneath all the things she was simultaneously thinking and not thinking, Mariposa touched on that old, unknowable orange. Her dream-orange, the orange she'd known, intuitively, from the start. Which she hadn't yet found.

But this. This was here. This hypnotic, expanding blue. Mariposa's blue heaven.

This time Marco didn't bother with his little aviator cap—who had time? With such a sublime new heaven calling. He did manage to grab his guitar, which had become an extension of himself, his Marco-guitar, as much a part of him as his arms or his chemically stunted legs. The guitar slung over his shoulder, Marco climbed on her back and slipped his plump little tadpole arms around her middle, at the spot where her upper and lower wings met.

"Ready?" Mariposa asked, though she had no idea where they were going, where she might fly them, other than into the blue.

The blue of not-knowing. It would be enough.

The cloud was growing. It was huge and blue and now tinged with bright pink in places. They launched into it and were immediately happy. It was almost a solid thing, this cloud, and it smelled, well, acrid and horrible, but Mariposa's head was soon buzzing pleasantly and she couldn't imagine anything could possibly be wrong except now, as they pushed through, she and Marco, pushing through that glorious, light-shedding blue, the cloud felt thicker and thicker. It was gritty, and now, it stung her eyes.

"Those fucking humans," she said.

"What? Oh, Miss Mariposa," he gasped, sounding for all the world like a school-boy once again. Mariposa flinched. So he knew. He knew she knew she wasn't really Marilyn Merlot. The charade was over, and while it still tore at Mariposa's heart—that he would want her to be anyone other than who she actually was, if only for a second. Mariposa wasn't into role play. She was who she fucking was. But, now, Marco seemed to know who she was, and was happy. In a way, it was like she had her Marco back. Her sweet, squishy Marco. They were flying through the most beautiful poison a heart could conjure, but Mariposa was so happy she could cry. Her Marco, returned to her.

"Isn't it wonderful?" he gasped. Then, as they flew deeper into the now-cloying blue, he started coughing, terrible racking coughs. He asked, "What? What did the stupid humans do?"

"It's a fucking insecticide cloud, Marco," she said, gasping now. Her flight wobbled, and she felt Marco's little body tense up.

"We have to land," Marco yelled. The wind had picked up, and now there were whips and whorls of shimmering colors all around them. "We have to land right now."

Mariposa coughed now, too, even more violently than Marco, and it felt as if her lungs were tearing apart. This hurt even more than a torn wing. She wrenched, and they dipped suddenly. She said, "We can't land, Marco. The thickest part of it is below us. We have to push on. Push through. We have to move on, Marco. I'm really sorry."

"We, uh, what?"

"I can fly us, Marco. I can fly us," Mariposa promised, even as she faltered, leaning too far to the left. "I just need to know where." Mariposa-no-longer-fucking-bimbo-Marilyn. She couldn't think. Her tiny butterfly brain thrummed with fatigue and fear and giveupitness.

Marco. Marco would have to make this decision.

"That's up to you, Marco. I want you to decide. Where do you want to go?"

Marco Goes
to the Cross Roots

Marco was not good at keeping secrets. "I am not good at keeping secrets," Marco said, speaking out loud, although he was walking alone. But secrets were what he was keeping. Ever since he told Mariposa she was really Marilyn Merlot, and the Blues had entered his life, well, the Blues had entered his life.

"The blues have entered my life," he spoke to the blade of grass he was passing. Marco did not like to keep secrets from Mariposa. On the other hand, secretions he liked, especially hers. "She has really incredible secretions," he said to the stick in the mud. He was living a lie.

"I am living a lie." He thought the stick in the mud had said something. He regretted telling Mariposa she was someone else. He had made a split second decision in the moment, and in the moment he thought it was a good decision, but the thing about decisions is sometimes you don't know how they're going to turn out. The decisions decide for themselves, or something like that.

"Decisions decide for themselves." The stick in the mud looked confused.

Marco thought these thoughts under the chilly moon of early morning as he was walking home from the late show at the Xanadew. The Xanadew Club was a hole-in-the bank club near a compost pile. Its close proximity to humans made it slightly dangerous and seedy. It smelled of ferment and decomposition, and contamination, which made it exciting and ripe for the Blues. It was a bit of a walk back to the Merlot pond and it gave Marco time to think. He walked alone, and thought all about the secrets he was secreting. He talked out loud to himself because that made them less like secrets. Mariposa would be asleep. An empty bottle would be by their moss bed.

"Mariposa will be asleep. An empty bottle will be by the bed. I love you, Mariposa. I am sorry I changed you."

Marco spoke to the wide sleeping universe that seemed to turn over in its sleep and if it heard Marco it only sighed in its vast sleepiness and indifference. He knew something had to change. He did not feel like the intrepid saver-of-the-day tadpolian hero, now he felt more like the jaded film noir slightly slimy private eye. The minute he had changed Mariposa into Marilyn, it had changed him into someone else.

He had only told her because he wanted her to be happy and he wanted her to have a good singing voice. "I just wanted her to be happy," Marco said to the leaf that fell at his tadpole feet.

"Marilyn Merlot just popped into my head, and now she won't even sing with me. She told me the Blues make her want to puke." So instead of the sexy, singing younger Marilyn, he had gotten the older, boozier, depressed Marilyn. But Marco needed the Blues because he had to keep from becoming a frog, and he couldn't tell Mariposa, and it was proving harder than he thought.

"I need the Blues," Marco told the leaf. Blind Catfish had taken him under his fin and taught him the guitar and he had become devoted to practicing, which drove a bit of wedge between him and Mariposa. Also, Blind Catfish Walkin' had hooked him up with Louie, Lou-y-a the Luna Moth, the apothecary, who was giving Marco a dull blue liquid that was part milkweed and ginseng with a dash of DDT, and some sort of mushroom. "It's the real deal," Marco told the pebble. It was a phrase that everyone used at the Xanadew. "The real deal." You have to tell a stone something twice.

"Louie Lou-y-a Moth said if I took this every day for two months I would stay a tadpole, but with arms and semi-functional legs. "I wouldn't be winning no 50 yard dashes, daddio." Marco said to the slug trail that shone iridescent in the early hours after midnight.

"That's how he talks," he added to the acorn. "But you can't miss any days because what you are taking is poison. If you miss, the poison will turn on you and you will die, and then you'll turn into a frog and what an ugly corpse you will be then, and we'll have to dig a bigger hole which will be a drag for everybody. Get my drift?" Marco got it. And at the end of two insect months divided by an amphibian year you'll go down to the crossroots and sell your tadpole soul to the devil who will come in the form of a rabbit and be dressed as a traveling salesman. Then and only then will he change you to where you won't change at all. Once a Marco always a Marco, x marcos the spot. But remember you won't be dancing the Charleston or the Jitterbug. Also, you'll get a free set of encyclopedias."

Marco spoke out loud so he wouldn't feel alone. All this had taken him away from Mariposa. He mentioned the jitterbug and it made him think of the dance lessons she was taking, and oh how he loved her, and though they still made love just as passionately as ever, something had gone out of it. She wasn't exactly Mariposa, and he wasn't exactly Marco; and he knew he had to change all that.

"I have to change all that," he told the babbling brook who never stopped babbling.

Tomorrow night was when he was supposed to go to the Crossroots to be changed, and once he was changed he could be honest with Mariposa and change her back to her old bitchy self as opposed to her now bitchy self, and he would tell her everything and everything would be good again. "Everything will be good again," he said to no one. Not even Marco was listening to himself now.

He knew he loved her now more than ever, and he hated they had grown apart. He hated that she was hanging around with this horsefly. "Horse's ass fly," Marco called him. He was a big mouth who called himself Pegasus. And then he'd turn on his side and call himself "the Black Stallion" just because he had flown too close to the bug zapper and it had turned him white on one side and charcoal black on the other side. Marco encouraged the horse fly to fly back to the bug zapper so he could get his other side burned white. He was a two-faced horse's ass and arrogant and boastful and Marco hated him.

The truth was, Marco was jealous. But he didn't have much justification to be jealous for he was hanging around with all sorts of seedy characters at the Xanadew club. It was weird. What he had learned was he only needed to be totally faithful to his guitar, his craft. At first, Blind Catfish Walkin' had introduced him to some of the local blues legends: B.B. Sting, and Howlin' Wolf Spider, and he was devoted to the purity of the Blues. Ironically though, the Blues attracted the worst kind of characters to the hole-in-the-bank venues Marco was playing. Pissants and stinkbugs, leeches and blood suckers

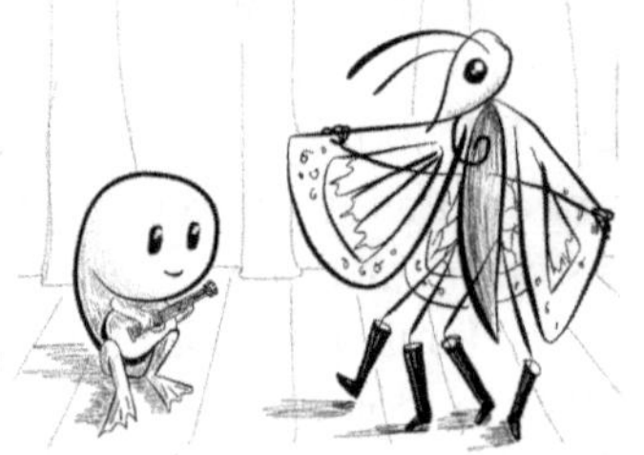

At the Xanadew.

of all kinds, dick ticks and horny heads, and Whorenets, and bitterflies and night crawlers, all sitting around the dark club drinking and taking pills. Shooting up with the needle in the haystack. He was hanging out with cockroaches, the porn stars of the insect world, and black widows, scorpions. He had to do it.

"I have to do it," he told the spider's web, illuminated by the lonely moon. He had no choice if he were to stay a tadpole. This is where he got his nightly concoction that made him float in and out of the music he was playing, and so the final irony. For in trying to stay the same, he was doing something that might forever change him. Marco was nearing his home. He stopped and lifted his little tadpole head—he was wearing a beret now because he was a Bluesman—and howled at the moon. A tadpole howling at the moon.

"It's the drugs," Marco sang to the tipsy moon.

When he arrived home by the old mill merlot pond, Mariposa was sleeping drunkenly on their mossy bed. Marco stashed his guitar in the corner and he squeezed in beside Mariposa and held her tightly. "My dear, dear, bitchy Mariposa. I will tell you the truth soon, maybe tomorrow, and you will be my Mariposa again, and we will fly this place forever." He kissed her and closed his eyes and dreamed of being in the same dream with her, that they were flying upward intoa beautiful blue cloud.

But then a rabbit dressed like a traveling salesman sucked up the blue cloud in his vacuum cleaner and told Marco that there were no seats left on Mariposa's dream tonight and he would have to be on standby. Marco woke up and chuckled a little at the absurdity of his dream and figured it was the concoction he was drinking, but not after tomorrow.

And just before he drifted back into his solo only dream, he remembered the little gas mask that the stink bug had given him when they journeyed together into the wormhole for the juice of the fungi. After they had returned to Xanadew, Marco had placed it in his guitar case.

The next day, Marco made Mariposa breakfast. Milkweed on toast. She went off to her dance lesson without saying much. Marco played his guitar and worked on a song:

I went down to the Crossroots, to sell my tadpole soul.

I went down to the Crossroots, to sell my tadpole soul.

I went down to the Crossroots and into the rabbit hole.

He went to the club early and set up and talked to the bartender, Betty the Barfly. The bumblebees rode in on their motorcycles and buzzed up to the bar, Blind Catfish squirmed in with Horny Head and Louie Lou-y-a Moth, the apothecary, and he motioned Marco over to their table. All the tables at the Xanadew club had six legs.

"Tonight's the night, Marco my boy," Blind Catfish said, leaning in. Marco stroked his goatee. He not only had a mustache, but because of the drug he was taking he now had a goatee.

"Are you ready, are you ready for the not changing," spoke the Moth who then rubbed his back legs together. "Meet me at the Crossroots at exactly midnight, insect standard time, not amphibian time. I'll be the Louie, Lou-y-a Moth by the side of the road. 'Oh baby we gotta go.' I'll have your last cup of Milkweed and ginseng with a dash of DDT, and then the devil will come up out of the rabbit hole, and he'll say something and then you'll say something. He'll have with him Frogzilla, an albino frog who didn't drink the poison properly. Don't look at him. He has sickly pink eyes and he'll turn you into an albino frog if you look him in the eye. The devil will test you. The devil will then play and tune your guitar and then he'll give it back to you. Then you'll be a tadpole forever with a tadpole soul and a bluesman's heart too.

"And don't forget the encyclopedias," added Marco.

"Right, and then he'll give you some encyclopedias. You know all this is fruitflyless, don't you?"

"What do you mean?" Marco asked.

"You're doing all this. Changing the very nature of your being because you think you love a butterfly. You want to be with a butterfly. Why don't you just fly into that bug zapper and get it over with… She has to leave you, you know? She has to fly to Mexico. Has she told you? Maybe she doesn't know yet either. But one day, she'll just up and fly away. She has to. I've known many Monarchs in my time, and they all flew away to Mexico, wherever that is, and none of them ever came back."

"But I love Mariposa with all my heart. It has to work out. It just has to. I'll go with her, or maybe there's a drug that will keep her from going." Marco spoke with a bit of panic in his voice.

"No," said the Moth. "There is no drug. She will leave you. She has to go."

"Then I will go with her. She loves me, and I love her. It's the only thing that is true in this world. It's the only thing that is real. It has to work. We've come too far to give up now."

"Whatever." Moth staggered off toward Betty the Barfly.

"Ready to play the Blues." Blind Catfish stood up and looked at Marco with his blind right eye and with his second sight made his way to the bandstand.

Betty Barfly brought Marco a drink. Tequila. He especially liked the worm at the bottom of the glass. It was an insect week night so it would be an early night. Marco packed up his guitar around eleven and left the club at 11:11 insect standard time. He walked on his ever weakening legs for a long time down the dark country lane and then turned onto a path with large hanging cypress trees until he came to the Crossroots. The place where two large roots like giant snakes crossed each other and made a perfect X. Just to the side of the cross roots was a large hole that was big enough to hold a rabbit or the devil.

Louie Lou-y-a Moth was there in his ghostly greenish wings against the darkness. "Here, drink this quickly, then take out your guitar and begin to play. Good luck, Tadpole, break a leg." And with that, Louie Lou-y-a the Luna Moth apothecary flew off in his ghostly way, disappearing into the darkness.

Marco opened his guitar case and began to play and sing:

Went down to the crossroots just to change my soul,

Went down the the crossroots just to change my soul.

Come up. Come up devil. I'm under your control.

Marco quickly drank the thick bluish liquid. It seemed darker and thicker than usual and immediately the world around Marco began to spin and pulsate with the vivid colors of hallucination. Marco looked at the black of the rabbit hole to try to contain the hallucinations. Suddenly, a sickly pale white ghost of a figure began to rise up out of the hole. He knew it was Frogzilla, the albino frog. It was hideous and Marco cast his eyes on the huge white stomach of the frog and then looked down at the hole again, careful not to look into the monster's eyes. Then springing out of the hole in a single bound was the rabbit devil dressed it a zoot suit who began to talk rapidly.

"Hello madam. Allow me to introduce myself. I am the devil of a deal and do I have a deal for you today. I'm the real deal. Get my drift, Tadpolio. I'm the whiz and nobody beats me. Tonight we have a sale on souls you won't believe and

I know you want to sell your soul to me and you happen to be in luck because we do take trade-ins and slightly used souls, particularly from little old ladies from Pasadena. This is my assistant, Frogzilla. Isn't he lovely. He has pink eyes. He tried to cheat me when he came to me as a tadpole and you see what happens when you try to cheat the devil. You get pink eyes and a misshapen white body. Say something, Frogzilla, so this little in-between-worlds tadpole will know you are real."

"I am the ghost of Christmas Past," Frogzilla monotoned.

Marco kept his gaze on the rabbit.

"He thinks he's in a Dickens novel. That's hell for you. It's different for everybody. Everybody gets scrooged. So let me get this straight. You want to be

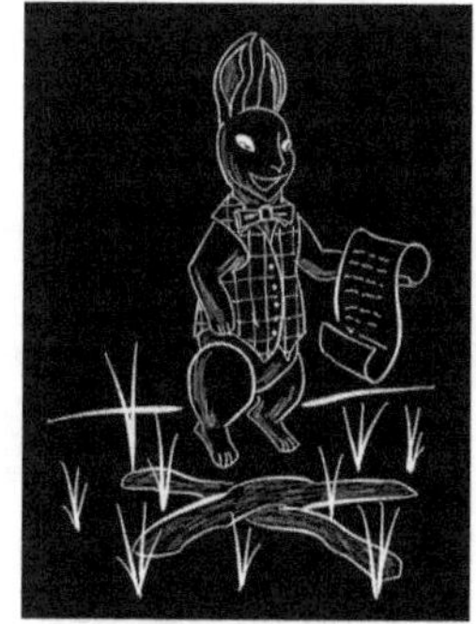

The Crossroots

a tadpole forever in exchange for your measly tadpole soul. You want me to stop what nature has invented and it just so happens to be your lucky day. We have a two for one sale, so for your soul I'll give you two tadpole souls and of course, with all sales over $19.99 you get a free set of encyclopedias. So what's it going to take to put you in one of these permanent tadpole souls with a one year guarantee? That's insect standard time, by the way. Here, the two souls we have left come in a nice pastel blue that will match your own little guitar there. So is it a deal?"

The devil rabbit talked so rapidly and convincingly that Marco only caught about half of what he said, but there was no going back now. This was the real deal. "Yes. It's a deal."

"You heard that, didn't you Frogzilla. You're the witness," the devil rabbit looked straight into Frogzilla's pink eyes.

"I am the ghost of Christmas present," monotoned Frogzilla.

"And there you have it. It's like a Christmas present you're getting, from the Easter bunny no doubt, and Jesus wept by God because he could never get a deal this good. Here, let me see your guitar." Marco handed the devil rabbit his blue guitar and the devil took it and tuned it quickly. He played a few notes that swirled around in the blue-tinted darkness and handed it back to Marco.

"There you go. Deal is done. Your tadpole soul is mine, and now you have two, and you'll stay just like you are until you are not, and when you are not you will be just like you are forever or until the warranty runs out on your souls and remember there are no returns. All sales are final. Get my drift?" And the devil rabbit bounded back down his hole as quickly as he had appeared.

Marco stood motionless, slightly bluer than before. And he looked at the feet of Frogzilla.

"I am the ghost of Christmas future," Frogzilla intoned and then floated slowly back down the rabbit hole. Marco turned away because he knew the sickly pink eyes would be the last thing to vanish.

There Marco stood, holding his guitar. The sky swirling in a pinkish darkness, and white milky clouds were gathering around the moon, and the night transforming reluctantly into morning was totally silent and still as if respecting the courage and audacity of such a tiny creature as Marco defying nature and the very universe itself. That amid all the vastness, and chaos and change, that love between two creatures was real.

"The realest thing in the universe," Marco said out loud as was his custom now. "This is the real real deal."

Marco took off his beret and flung it as far as he could into the remaining darkness. He threw back his little bare head and Marco howled at the moon… "Ah whooooo!"

When Marco got back home, he put his guitar away. It was almost sunrise, and Mariposa stirred uneasily out of her sleep when Marco squeezed in beside her.

"Where have you been?" Mariposa asked sleepily, and she spoke as Mariposa not Marilyn.

"I've been down to the Crossroots," Marco said solidly. "I have a lot to tell you. I have a confession to make, Marilyn." He sighed morosely, and Mariposa squeezed his squishy little tadpole hand.

"Don't," she said. "I'm scared. We are too close to humans here. Something terrible happened tonight. Ed (that's the horsefly Marco hated) came over and we were drinking and he was telling me all about the rodeo and how he would take me sometime and he was buzzing about in his loud way, and suddenly a giant flyswatter came down and squashed him flat. That was Ed's last ride." Mariposa looked at Marco. "Why are you smiling, Marco? It was fucking terrible."

"Sorry, Marilyn. But I have a lot to tell you. I think I've made a terrible mistake."

Mariposa kissed Marco and climbed on top of him because they both loved to have morning sex, but this time it was different and he stopped Mariposa.

"Mariposa, I mean Marilyn, I mean Mariposa, I mean…I don't know what I mean. I have to tell you something."

"Oh Marco."

And as Marco looked up toward the pinkish morning sky a strange but beautiful blue cloud was coming toward them. It filled up half the sky in its blueness like some blue heaven come to rescue them. And now again Marco was faced with a split second decision. Would this be wrong too? But they had to fly this place. They had to leave here.

"Fly me into that," Marco said.

Marco grabbed his guitar and climbed on Mariposa's back, slipping his plump little tadpole arms around her middle, at the spot where her upper and lower wings met.

"Ready?" Mariposa asked with a dash of apprehension in her now Mariposa voice. Into the blue of not knowing. It would be enough.

They ascended into its blueness and pinkness and for a few minutes felt a sudden euphoria. But as they flew deeper into the cloud, it became thicker and it stung Marco's eyes and burned his throat. What was this?

"Those fucking humans," Mariposa said, coughing as she spoke.

"What did the fucking humans do?"

"It's a fucking insecticide cloud, Marco." Marco loved the way Mariposa said the word "fucking" and he knew for sure she was back to her old self. He wondered how? The sudden ingestion of insecticide or perhaps she had been pretending to be Marilyn.

Focus! Marco, focus! Marco would never know if he and Mariposa didn't get out of this cloud, and soon.

"We have to land," Marco yelled. The wind had picked up and now there were whips and whorls of shimmering colors all around them. "We have to land now."

Mariposa coughed violently. Marco knew she would be unconscious soon. He would have longer, for he was an amphibian and the pesticides would take longer to incapacitate him.

"We can't land, Marco. The thickest part of it is below us. We have to push through. I can fly us, Marco, I can fly us." Even though Marco knew she couldn't. She coughed again and they swerved far to the left and Marco nearly fell off. Marco could see Mariposa's eyes were nearly swollen shut.

"I just need to know where. That's up to you, Marco. You have to decide. Where do you want to go?"

"Mexico, Mariposa, Mexico." Marco said resolutely even though the insecticide was getting to him as well. He was Marco Fucking Tad Polo and he had been to the Crossroots and he was now transformed into a being that could love Mariposa until they died, but dying right now was not an option.

"Think, Marco, think. Focus, Marco, focus," he said out loud.

Then Marco remembered the little gas mask the stink bug had given him. He slung the guitar off his shoulder and pulled it out of the case.

"Here, Mariposa, put this on over your face. Close your eyes and just keep flapping your wings and I will steer us up. We need to go up and try to get above the blue cloud. If they're trying to kill insects then the cloud probably doesn't go up too far."

He helped Mariposa on with the little gas mask, and he could tell it was working, that she was able to breath as her wings straightened and he pulled up on the back of her head and they ascended. But now Marco couldn't see and he was losing his breath. He tried to cough it out, but he was feeling light-headed and they were still in the cloud. He began to think of the pink eyes of the albino frog, and he thought about looking into them and he was letting go, letting go, letting go.

When suddenly he felt something lift him up as if something had him by the collar and they rose and rose until Marco opened his eyes and they were in the clear sky of morning. He could see the poisonous cloud below him and he wondered if he and Mariposa had died and this was all just a dream. He slowly lifted the gas mask off Mariposa's face and she looked up at him in bewilderment. Her wings had stopped moving but they were flying steadily forward now above the clouds. Then they heard a voice:

"I am the Early Bird, and I always get the worm."

It was the Early Bird. The Early Bird had saved them. "My little friends. I see you have survived this long, but you were about to meet your end at the hands of the awful humans and their poison gas. Lucky for you I was out eating panicked insects flying away from the gas. You have to get up pretty early in the morning to beat the Early Bird."

Marco and Mariposa couldn't believe their good fortune. "Thank you, Early Bird. We're leaving but we don't know where to go. Can you help us?" Mariposa asked, still coughing some from the effects of the gas.

"Well, for a butterfly and her passenger there's really only one direction. I'll fly you up a little higher and you can catch the jet stream. It only blows one direction but it will carry you safely as far as it goes... Now if you'll excuse me, I am the Early Bird and I have some worms to catch."

He ascended a little higher and released Mariposa and Marco into the stream, into the river of wind that carried them effortlessly. They floated for hours across the broad fields and meadows, and it was not the false blue cloud, but a real blue heaven with the endless sky above them and the river of wind carrying them. First, they made love on the wind and it was heavenly bluish and weightless and bluish and Mariposa had 117 orgasms and Marco had four which was a record for him, and then they slept on the wind and for the first time in a long time, they slept in the same dream, and it felt like the true blue heaven.

Then Marco told Mariposa everything, and how he was really sorry he told her the lie of Marilyn Merlot, and that he only wanted her to be a good singer because he thought that would make her happy, and that her real singing voice was really pretty awful, but now that he played guitar he thought he might be able to teach her to sing. He told her about the concoction and Louie, lou-y-a the Luna moth, and going down to the Crossroots and meeting the devil and Frog-zilla, and how the devil was a rabbit dressed like a traveling salesman. He told her everything as the river stream of wind carried them along.

"But we have to go back," Marco suddenly said.

"Why, Marco, why do we have to go back?"

"I forgot my encyclopedias," Marco giggled. Marco thought he had a very good sense of humor.

"Oh Marco," Mariposa laughed like the old Mariposa. She thought Marco's sense of humor was sexy. "I think I can go for 118, and I need to get you to five."

She kissed Marco as they hit some mid-air turbulence which only made the love making more erotic.

But there was one secret Marco held back. One little secret. He did not tell Mariposa he had sold his soul to the devil. He didn't even know what that meant. He had his new bluish soul now that would keep him a tadpole for a long time and he even had a back-up soul stored in his guitar case. Wrapped in that second soul was a paper the devil had given him and he had signed it. Just business stuff. Just procedural stuff, the devil assured him. No need to read the fine print. And if you can't trust the devil who can you trust. Focus, Marco, focus. Focus on the now. The pleasure of the moment as Mariposa goes into the spasms of 118 and yes, yes, yes, yes, yes, and Marco hits number five. Good job, Marco.

Butterfly in the Mexico
of her Childhood Dreams

Mariposa closed her butterfly eyes and screamed. It was the most wonderful thing, to make love to Marco on a gushing stream of wind, the sky blue and endless above them, the world, with its disgusting humans and weird blind catfish and gossiping insect-mamas and that slutty barfly far below them. The insecticide cloud, as beautiful and dangerous as the bug zapper, had weakened her, but Marco was flying high in more ways than one. Now, with every thrust, he giggled like a little boy and gasped, oh, geez, oh, oh geez, all of his blues mumbo jumbo momentarily forgotten. He reached orgasm number five, and Mariposa, soaring on past 118, 119, 120..., held Marco tight. She was falling a bit more in love with him with every passing moment—with every pharmaceutically-enhanced Marco-chuckle—now that she was returned to Mariposa. Oh, it was the most wonderful thing, to be who she was. Who she really fucking was.

And Marco, funny, sweet, sexy Marco. Something about him was more Marco-ish than ever before. He seemed so happy, though, oddly more bluish than ever before. He almost blended into the sky, and Mariposa couldn't figure out why. It couldn't just be the blues music; life was rarely that literal, even inside insect fables.

They flew on, over patches of green and brown and gray, over little silver ribbons of highway with their tiny automobiles, like ants, crawling across. Over blue pools of water, over baseball diamonds and school bus holding lots. They were post-coital now—or, more likely, between-coitals—holding each other tight. Mariposa sighed. Marco had told her he could teach her how to sing. This both terrified her and thrilled her. It was a frightening thing for Mariposa, to offer her singing voice over for someone's examination, and she feared that kind of scrutiny. And yet, this was her Marco. Her dear sweet Marco. If she could be vulnerable with anyone, it was him.

And perhaps, maybe. Maybe, he could help her. Maybe her sweet tadpole lover and his sweet little guitar really could teach her how to sing.

In her heart of hearts, she knew how horrible her singing voice was. And, even deeper, into her heart of hearts of hearts, she feared this was just the beginning. That there was plenty of horrible inside her. That the only thing she really had to offer the world was a pair of pretty wings.

And how much longer would that last? She had already been torn and scorched. The beautiful orange of her wings—an orange which seemed to exude its very own light—had begun to fade since, it seemed, the very moment she had her wings, her first emerging from her cocoon—her months of darkness. And the fading had been progressing at a much faster rate now, since her encounter with the bug zapper. Marco insisted her wings were just as beautiful now as they had always been, but what else could he say? He was a sweet tadpole. And, he loved her. He could hardly even see her faults anymore. To Marco's love-struck eyes, her imperfections did not even exist.

But Mariposa couldn't quite believe that she could ever actually be all-the-way happy. True happiness frightened her. Being happy meant there always lurked the possibility of losing that happiness. Something would have to go wrong. And something wronger than simply not knowing where in the hell they were going.

She considered asking Marco, though she doubted he would know. Marco was a sweet tadpole, and he was a handsome tadpole, he was a motherfucking sexy tadpole, but he was not very forward-looking tadpole. She had tried when she made him pick the place. To choose. And he had. Mexico. Mexico.

Of course, Mariposa had heard stories about Mexico. She was a monarch butterfly, after all. Mexico was the setting of every butterfly fairy tale. In Mexico, the days were full of the soft breezes for playing all the butterfly games. The nights were sweet-smelling and made of clear and perfect violet-colored skies. A butterfly could only dream sweet dreams under such a sky. Tiny stars dripped down like rain, landing softly on the lids of every sleeping butterfly. There was every kind of flower in Mexico and the nectar in each and every one was candy-sweet. In Mexico, no butterfly ever aged. In Mexico, you could fly as high you wanted without getting dizzy or tired. In Mexico, a butterfly's wings never sagged with age. In Mexico, butterflies never aged at all.

Her mother had told her that such a place didn't exist. Mexico, her mother had scoffed. Nobody believes in Mexico.

They were flying over desert now, the earth beneath them yellow-brown, sun-scorched, and cracked. This hardly looked like the lush green hills of her childhood's nighttime stories. Mariposa was worried: where were they going?

"Marco," Mariposa began. "What made you think of Mexico? As a place for us to fly to? Where did you even hear of it?" She thought perhaps she had mentioned Mexico during one of her late-night drunken babbles. Mariposa was bad for that, for babbling endlessly and way too honestly late at night when she'd had too much Merlot, or, back in the day, too much bourbon-infused nectar. Or, it could be she had mentioned Mexico in her sleep. Marco said she did that sometimes, sighed aloud her longings while she slept.

The earnest young tadpole answered immediately. "Louie, Lou-y-a Luna moth told me. He said every Monarch butterfly has to fly to Mexico." Marco, still holding on tight to Mariposa's wings, shrugged. "I figured I would just go with you." He paused a second, remembering something. "Oh, and Betty the Barfly said they have lots of tequila in Mexico. Yummy, yummy tequila."

"Betty the fucking Barfly," Mariposa mumbled under her breath. Out loud, she said, "Oh, Marco. I'm afraid they were lying to you. Just putting you on." The desert below them had begun to lift itself up into little ripples of brown with bits of scrubby green tucked in here and there.. "Oh, Marco. You always believe everyone is so good inside. Some people just aren't good."

Marco was quiet a moment, then said. "Yeah, like Ed, the Horse's Ass, for example."

Mariposa sighed. "Oh, Marco. You silly, sweet tadpole. Ed was fun to drink with, but, oh, you are the only one for me."

But something else was bothering her. Mariposa had never known Marco to own a set of encyclopedias, or even to show any interest in owning such a thing. Actually, she wasn't even sure anyone even sold encyclopedias anymore. She had laughed when he said it. Marco was never sexier to her than when he was cracking a joke or subjecting her to one of his terrible puns. But now, the whole thing perplexed her.

"Marco," she asked, after a pause. "You said you forgot your set of free encyclopedias." Of course, he'd never said they were free. Mariposa was going on a hunch. "What did you buy? I mean, surely the horrible little devil-rabbit would not just give you anything. The devil is not known for his generosity."

"Hmmm," Marco began. "That is a very good question." Mariposa turned around to look at him. He looked slightly horrified.

"Is it?" Mariposa asked. Despite her worries over their destination, it felt wonderful now to be held inside the wind. The wind a kind of cocoon, but a welcoming one. Hardly the stifling black confinement of Mariposa's adolescence. She wanted to relax, but there was a knot of worry in her stomach. Marco was a horrible liar; even if Mariposa really had lost her memory she wasn't sure she really would have believed him when he called her Marilyn Merlot. But that whole incident seemed to weigh on him so heavily. He had felt such remorse at his deception. What could he possibly be hiding from her now?

"I bought a birthday present for you." Marco gave an awkward, fake-sounding laugh. "I didn't want to tell you what it was."

"A birthday present? For me?" Mariposa was incredulous. "Marco," she asked, "When is my birthday?"

She was sure she'd never told him, and the reason she was sure of this was because she herself had no idea when her birthday was. Butterflies hate to be reminded of things like birthdays and the passing of time. They didn't keep records of such things and certainly never stored a specific date in their memories.

The knot of worry in Mariposa's stomach clenched itself still tighter. She was, for a moment, in terrible pain and she held her breath. But then, the pain eased off, just a little, and Mariposa exhaled. She was waiting for Marco to answer her.

"Umm..." Marco began. He was literally squirming, trying to come up with an answer, and Mariposa relented. Obviously, whatever it was he had purchased, he was embarrassed about. She wondered if it was a new pair of shoes. Mariposa loved shoes, and not just sexy white go-go boots, made for walking. She would love to see what Marco would pick out for her to wear on her feet. Feet can be incredibly sexy if you knew how to dress them. Especially if they were the only part of you you dressed. Or, perhaps, she reasoned, it was a sex toy. That would explain Marco's clumsy attempts at subterfuge. The poor blue tadpole was embarrassed. A sex toy. Mariposa had to admit, she found the idea intriguing, fake birthday or not. And a sex toy from the devil? Well, that had to be good...

"Never mind," Mariposa said. "I'm sorry. I don't want to spoil the surprise. You are such a sweet tadpole. I love you."

"Oh, Mariposa." The beautiful tadpole sighed. "I love you. So, so much."

She had felt such relief to not have to pretend to be Marilyn Merlot anymore, but now that she was her old self again, she felt uncertain. It was as if she couldn't remember how to act like herself. Or, worse: it was as if she didn't even know who she was. Mariposa sighed. This long, easy flying lent itself to periods of deep contemplation. Back during her caterpillar days, she was simply voracious. All she could do was eat and eat and eat. There was no thinking at all to be done then. And then, while sleeping in the cocoon, she could only dream. And dream she did. She dreamt of glittering lights and dressing rooms full of flowers and fine European chocolates rolled in coconut flakes and milkweed pollen and dance clubs full of loud music that would throb through her ribcage, that she would still be able to feel, like a heartbeat, after everything was over and she lay in some glamorous high rise apartment somewhere trying to sleep. Except, then, when she was finally all the way formed—all grown up and ready to go—she would fly out in the world and never have to sleep again.

That was the dream: to enjoy life so much she never wanted to pause, never wanted to rest. It was exhausting just to dream that way, though. Let alone to try to live it.

Mariposa was about to really slip away, into the dark melancholy that had been beckoning her from her very hungry caterpillar days, when Marco, who had saved the day now, in his sweet-Marco way so many times, once again called her out of danger. This time, an even more unreachable and dangerous place than ever before. This time, the unreachable and dangerous place was Mariposa's own dark soul.

The blue of not-knowing, which maybe, Mariposa thought, wasn't blue at all. Maybe it was the purple of not knowing—those oft dreamed of fairy-tale Mexico nights—or the black of not knowing. What everything was, really, when you turned off the light.

And, now, she was certain of it. She really did have a tummy ache. Though the discomfort, the tightening, had moved to the upper half of her thorax.

"Mariposa!" Marco was yelling, too loudly in her ear. Excitable little tadpole, though at least the insecticide-cloud high had worn off. He was, at least, a fully conscious and in-the-moment tadpole, at the moment. "Look! Look! Down below!"

Mariposa looked. Down below.

"Oh, Marco," she gasped. "It's so beautiful."

Even as she spoke, she felt them losing elevation, but slowly, gently. Mariposa gasped again. There was no danger here. Below them, a place that was coming to them, swiftly but smoothly. It was as if Mariposa, terrible pilot she was, was not flying them at all. And then, she remembered: she wasn't. This was the wind. Some beautiful benevolent wind landing them gently on the lush green hills below. The air was just as sweet as the place of her dreams, and the sun just as soft and perfect.

"Could it be?" Mariposa was so taken with the sight before her, below her, that she forgot how much she hated it when a person said a thought aloud. She had, in all her butterfly years, despised such a habit, finding it incredibly annoying. But now, in her happiness, she did not mind annoying herself, or anyone else. She said, "Oh Marco! It is! It really is—it's Mexico!"

They were so happy, they both moved simultaneously into position. If thank-god-we're-still-alive sex was amazing, and we're-about-to-die sex was electrifying, then, we've-found-fucking-paradise-sex is, well, heavenly. And so, they loved and loved and landed in Mexico, aka the Promised Land, trying to catch their breaths.

"I am so fucking happy," Mariposa said as they rose to their feet and took in the sight around them. Sweetly feathered bits of yellow sunshine touched every blade of grass, every tree. But even as she said it, the pain bloomed across her back and she nearly doubled over in pain.

"Oh, Mariposa, I'm so glad—oh, Mariposa," Marco said, realizing Mariposa was not doing well, "What's wrong, my love? Oh, we need to find you a doctor."

But Mariposa knew, in a sudden, terrifying flash of knowing, understood just what the problem was. And as she dropped to the soft grass in hers and Marco's just-found paradise, she thought she glimpsed, in the corner of her eye, a flash of fuzzy white bob past, several yards behind Marco who was kneeling now beside her. He picked up her hand and kissed it. The flash of white—Mariposa was certain now she was hallucinating—was a rabbit. Wearing a tweed vest. And smiling. A rabbit carrying a briefcase. From her confusion, from her pain, a band of sickly green light wrapping itself around her eyes so she could barely see Marco, let alone the rabbit-that-just-might-be-the-devil lurking behind.

She remembered. She remembered what the mothers back at the pond had said, about what sort of a disgusting creature a tadpole and a butterfly's copulation might result in. She remembered the other piece about Mexico, the fairyland, what her mother had said wasn't true.

Mexico, the roosting place. The egg-laying place. The towering trees all around them.

"Marco," she began. She closed her eyes. This couldn't be happening. "I—"

But here she stopped, for when she opened her eyes to explain to Marco what was happening—the real reason they had been brought here, by biological instinct and butterfly magic—she saw, in a distance, a splotch of orange. Orange like fire, but prettier. Orange stark against the blue, blue sky.

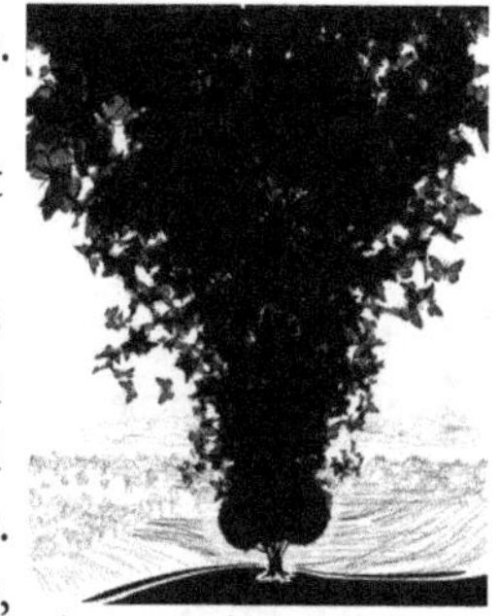
The great butterfly soul.

It was the great butterfly soul. She needed to be a part of that. She would leave everyone, and everything to become a part of the living tree of butterflies. So close. So very close.

The blue of not-knowing. No. It was orange. The place she was supposed to be. The being she was supposed to join.

Marco: Mad as Adam

I'm going to have babies, Marco… Marco babies… I'm scared, Marco, what will they look like?"

"Babies? Little Caterpoles. Little Tadpillars… Don't worry. They'll look like you. Maybe a little darker. Better swimmers. But they'll look like you."

He embraced Mariposa and she climbed on top of him and they made we-just-made-babies-love.

"Here let me show you the Mexican cartwheel," Mariposa cried out as she began to grind on Marco.

Mariposa orgasmed 15 or twenty times—little winged spasms of pleasure. Marco was still working on number one when he felt Mariposa go rather lifeless. He continued to do his little tadpole thrusts, tadpole vaults, but Mariposa was unresponsive. He looked up, and she seemed to be in a trance. She was staring into the great orange pulsating mass of Monarchs in a single tree almost completely buried in a sea of Monarch butterflies.

"It's the one great soul. The tree of life," she hypnotically intoned. "They're calling to me, Marco. I have to go. The one great soul is calling to me."

Marco strained to listen while continuing to thrust, but he didn't hear a soul. Marco closed his eyes and kept thrusting, but how can one poor humping tadpole compete with the one great soul in all its crowded oneness.

"I have to go, Marco. It's my destiny."

Marco kept thrusting and thrusting until he went limp. The one great soul puts a lot of pressure on a fellow.

"I thought Broadway was your destiny. Is this Broadway? It is the bright lights for sure. Is Broadway in there? Are there cigarettes and bourbon infused nectar in there?"

Marco was being ironic, as intelligent tadpoles seem to be, but it was lost on Mariposa. It is hard to get bemused irony across to someone who is in a hypnotic trance. If sex, alcohol, and cigarettes could not dissuade Mariposa then all might be lost. She lifted off of Marco like a helicopter taking off and flew right into the one great soul. She just flew directly into it like it was some hippie bug zapper. He couldn't look long. It was like looking while flying too close to the sun. All that orange and orange red, and orange pink, and orange orange pulsating and glowing like a crayon orgy. And then Mariposa was gone. Swallowed up by a cloud of brilliant wings. What could he do? Just like that. Faster than you can say

Aztec gold, or fuchsia, or henna. She was gone.

Then a voice from the whiteness behind him spoke in a slightly familiar voice. "Yo Bozo boy! Beautiful isn't it, my boy? It reminds me of Hell. Oh, don't think hell is a dull place. All the great artists end up there. Selling their souls one way or another. It's filled with color and lights and starry nights and the persistence of memory and melting colors and we have our own disco ball. It's groovy." It was the devil rabbit himself dressed dandily in a white tweed suit.

"It looks like you may have lost your lover. The very lover you sold your soul to me for, if I'm not mistaken, and I never am. Too bad I don't accept returns."

"She'll come back. I'll find her," said Marco, still shaken by her sudden departure and the devil's sudden arrival. "I'll find her," He repeated.

"Maybe you will—maybe you won't. Devil never even lived. Forwards backwards. I'm just here to pick up some colorful souls and wings to decorate hell, and oh yes, Tequila. What would hell be without Tequila. It would be like… well…hell, I guess."

"Excuse me. I have to go into the one great soul now. To find Mariposa." Marco started to get up.

"Not even the devil wants any part of the one great soul. It's a scam anyway. Smoke and mirrors. Just millions of butterfly sheep following their excretions and instinct. They're like humans. The worst insult in bugdom. Followers following the following. One great soul my devil's behind. It can kiss my forked tail. Hibernation? Are you kidding me? Sleeping like you're dead. What a waste of death. It pisses me off. I'm into hypernation. Pins and needles. Pain, Marco. Bed of nails pain. That's where it's at." The devil paused his rant.

"Mariposa is going to have my babies."

"Do you mean my babies?" The devil rabbit smiled whitely.

"Excuse me?" asked Marco. "What do you mean?"

"My babies…The fine print. When you sold me your soul. Page 126, paragraph 66: The party of the first part…"

"I didn't agree to that. That's not fair." Marco cried.

"You should never trust the devil…but I'll tell you what I'm going to do. I need a favor. If you take the extra soul I gave you and unfold it, it will reveal a map, a revealing map, and if you can unlock the code in the one great soul and find your Mariposa then you can keep your kids. Who needs any more stinking kids in hell. I hate kids. Little devils running around. I just want someone to fool the stupid one great soul." And with that the devil skipped off down the road.

Marco was despondent. He opened the guitar case and pulled out the extra soul and unfolded it

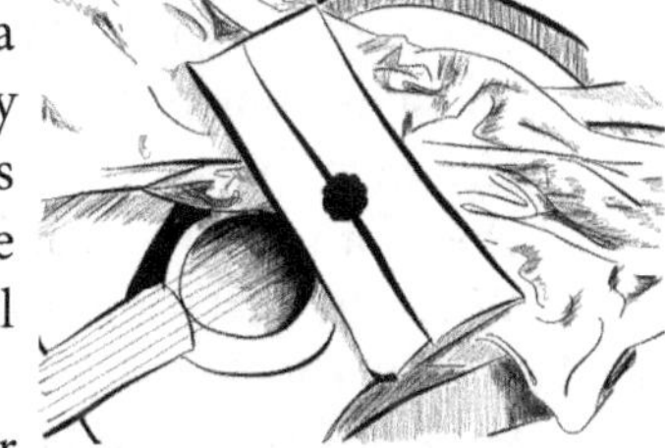

the fine print.

and laid it on top of his guitar case. He also took out the crumpled contract he had signed and tried to read the fine print. He squinted and squinted until his squinter was broken. He put the soul back into his guitar case and he started off toward the one great soul that shone like a bright sun directly in front of him.

One great soul or one great hole, Marco moved toward the pulsating mass of butterflies. As he got closer, the mass seemed to be rotating counter-clockwise, throbbing brightly in and out, out and in, clockwork orange, he was in front of it now. He was looking for a lever to pull. He was a born lever puller. There was no lever. If it was one great soul, shouldn't there be one great entrance? Thoughts like a race car went through Marco's brain. Would it swallow him up?

"Will it swallow me up?" asked Marco. "Will I be able to see and maneuver? How will I find Mariposa? Is there an admission charge?" Marco stood before the one great soul in the tree of life and he opened his guitar case. He took out the extra soul he had and as the devil told him he unfolded it. And when he did, it began to pulsate in its blackness and a map appeared. Not a map really.

"It's not a map really," said Marco. "More a kaleidoscope of words and symbols. It reminds me of how Mariposa used to diagram sentences in the sky."

And when he said that he felt a deep pang of loneliness for Mariposa. Do you know what a deep pang feels like? Can you, oh reader, remember when you were so deep in love with the impossible, or you missed someone so badly, and then you see or hear something that reminds you of that person, and that feeling in your gut hits you and you stare off into space awhile, like right now. I hope you do. Anyway, that's how Marco felt. He remembered the first time he was trying to diagram a sentence in the sky. His mind became cloudy, and he was on the ladder, and a semicolon knocked him off and he fell to the ground and Mariposa stood over him like a punctuation angel, and said, "Bad semicolon, bad!" and then she helped Marco up and he could feel her sweet breath on his slimy little cheek. He had fallen groundward and skyward at the same time.

But now Marco had to focus on a map of words that couldn't even focus on itself. The map was like a watery canvas with letters and symbols floating and swirling about like blind tadpoles. Finally the words began to form like synchronized tadpoles. The first words said, To idiot. Well, Marco didn't like that. "Dammit I'm mad," he said. And Marco was. "Bad map, bad, bad map," Marco wagged his finger. Then another phrase appeared as if some sort of cryptic message. It said, In words alas drown I. That message then was instantly replaced with. Daedalus: nine peninsula: dead.

And then the soul screen went black. Blank. Marco blinked. Blank. Black. He reached for the remote and remembered where he was.

"What the fuck does that mean? And two damn colons. Semicolon's ugly brother. Stack cats."

Marco thought and he thought until his thinker broke. "Nine somethings. Daedalus." He remembered something from school. One of the sky sentences. "Wings. Too close to the sun. His son. The sun. Dead. Daedalus. They died.

Peninsula."

This was too many for him. Marco needed a break. Broken thinker, broken squinter. He picked up the one extra soul, turned it upside down, and shook it like an etch-a-sketch, or a magic 8-ball, but it revealed only one more message. It read: Go to the nearest Chinese restaurant and get an egg roll and a fortune cookie.

"What's Chinese?" Marco wondered. The extra soul was not helping.

Marco had to figure out how to get into the swirling counterclockwise moving mass of millions of Monarchs, sleeping, dreaming, dreaming, sleeping one great soul of a dream. How to get high enough into the tree of life. Suddenly, something tapped him on his little tadpole shoulders. Marco was getting a little wary of things coming up from behind him. He turned around expecting to see the devil rabbit, but instead it was a small black bird who cowered as if fearful of Marco.

"Who are you?" asked Marco.

"I'm the Scared Crow," came the hoarse but tiny voice.

"A crow? You're awfully small. You look more like a black wren. Are you the wren man?"

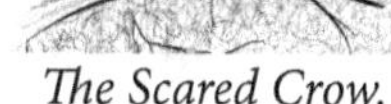

"My mother ate a Monarch butterfly by mistake when she was pregnant with me. It stunted my growth, and she abandoned me here. I was raised by a Wren mother. I have a nervous condition that makes me afraid of everything. I guess I'm both the Scared Crow and the Wren man…Would you

The Scared Crow.

like a guided tour of the one great soul? I have one leaving in ten minutes."

"Well, yes, I was trying to find my way in. I'm looking for someone. So you can fly me into it?"

"Oh yes. Show you the sights. There's a whole city in there. And a road."

"Is there a peninsula?" asked Marco, hopefully.

"What's a peninsula? Like a spider? I'm afraid of spiders."

"I don't know. I have this map." Marco showed the Scared Crow his map and a new message appeared. "I saw crow-Orca was I."

"What does that mean?"

"I don't know. Maybe Orca is the name of a peninsula." Then a new message appeared: "I'm a lasagna, bang a salami."

"What the hell does that mean? What's a salami?"

"I don't know. It must be trying to tell me something."

"Yes. That you need a new soul. Well, if we see a salami inside we'll ask it. Alright, are you ready to go?"

"I think so." Marco climbed on his back, just above the wings of the little black scared crow.

"Pull up if I pull up," instructed the crow.

"Okay, I'm ready."

And they flew straight away into the blinding, throbbing mass of butterfly wings and into the mirror rim and it opened up like the garage doors to the tunnel of love, a funnel cake of carnival sounds between the space caps and stack cats.

"Don't be afraid," shouted the Scared Crow.

"Aren't you afraid?" Marco shouted back.

"Of course, I am. I'm terrified. But that's my job." Scared Crow landed on a limb inside the one great soul. "Here's our first stop…The Limbpire State Building to give you an overview of the one great soul."

Marco looked down through the mass of the millions. Down below them in the center seemed to be a giant screen projecting something. It looked like a giant movie screen.

"What is that?" asked Marco.

"That's where we're headed next," replied Scared Crow. "It's the nexus of the universe. It's where time meets. Forward, backwards. It's Times Squared." Scared Crow then flew down into the maddening crowd of color and lights and noises.

"Why is it so loud? How can they sleep?"

"Yeah. It's a cawcaphony." The crow caw cawed. "In Times Squared every dream that has ever been dreamed is projected on these giant screens simultaneously. The energy to project these dreams are provided by the youngest monarchs pedaling on a bicycle built for a million, pedaling deep in the one great soul that turns a dynamo that projects all the dreams on all these screens.

"The next stop is Broadway. The Adam and Eve fountain near Strawberry Hills next to the Tree of Life."

"Never odd or even," said Marco out loud.

"Hang on to your salami," said the Scared Crow.

"The story goes," continued Scared Crow, "that a small fountain sprang out of the trunk of the elephant tree. Sleeping monarchs formed a mosaic of two humans with Monarch wings, and inscribed on the tree it said, 'Madam in Eden I am Adam.' And in here, everything flows backwards, falls upwards. Adam and Eve is where the world ends. A space caps comes down and takes Adam and Eve away, and all the life on earth thrives. The end is the beginning."

"Exactly. Salami."

"It all starts at the end. The beginning."

"The beginning of the end."

"No. just the beginning—after the end."

"Heads or tails?"

"Always heads."

"Now back to Times Squared to meet Dr. Awkward. The Lizard of Ooze."

"Ah."

"Not Ah—ooze."

They flew back down from Times Squared to a small muddy stream. The

Scared Crow spoke: "The older Monarchs are sleeping here. This is where your Mariposa is I suspect. But the chance of finding her is slim and none. And she's no nun. There are a hundred thousand or so sleeping here, give or take a hundred thousand…Look, there he is. The Lizard of Ooze."

On the bank lay a small brown spotted lizard with wings. Around him towered dreamscapes and they were at the center of the one great soul. The tree of life where the beginning and the end meet in the middle. The place where every story, false or true, flows from. And Marco could see every dream that had ever been dreamed on giant screens the size of four leaf clover leaves, being driven by sleeping monarchs on bicycles built for a million. "East side, west side all around the town."

"Wheels are circles," said the lizard of Ooze. "And circles are wheels."

Marco listened as he watched the giant screen of dreams, of every dream that had ever been dreamed and in a blink of a flash he thought he saw Mariposa and him flash by.

"Hallucination," he said aloud.

"No. It's real. Here is real. Outside of this is the hallucination. Dreams are the only real thing. Devil never even lived."

"Okay," interrupted Scared Crow. "That concludes the tour of the one great soul. I hope you have enjoyed it and will come back sometime. You'll exit out through the one great soul gift shop and out through the tunnel of time. I'll leave you here and you'll be escorted out by the Finch. Just make sure it is the Good Finch and not the Bad Finch. The finch always wears plaid. Also, it appears there is a storm coming, so take care. The humans have cut down much of the forests around the preserve, so we have little protection here now from storms. So take care and be safe." And Scared Crow flew off.

"Now off to your right are sleeping older Monarchs, many of these are pregnant and will lay their eggs as they start to fly back north. Many will die," spoke a plaid-wearing Finch. Marco wandered and walked among the sleeping hum of softly fluttering wings. These Monarchs dreamed privately—away from the bustle of Times Squared. He stepped carefully among the flightless wings and looked into the sleeping faces as the voice of the Good Finch trailed off into silence.

Marco stopped and listened carefully to the soft murmur of dreams being almost imperceptibly transmitted through Monarch antennae. As a musician, Marco had learned to listen to dreams like they were diminished chords—harmony and dissonance. Now he caught the faint scent of nectar-infused bourbon with a trace of Ginseng, and stale cigarette smoke, and he followed it until it became stronger. Harmony. Dissonance. Bluesman. Jazzman. Ninth chord. He passed a few dead Monarchs. Daedalus: nine, peninsula: dead. The sleeping, dreaming monarchs narrowed into what? A peninsula. The smell and hum grew stronger. Until it was a whole hum. Ginseng. Bug zapper, a hundred orgasms, a siren's song, karaoke, east side, west side, all around the town, and he found her.

Mariposa was sleeping at the end point or the beginning point of the peninsula. He had found her by the scent of her dreams—calling him; and he lay down beside her and felt the whole world fold into them, into their dream.

"Dreams are the only real thing," Marco said as was his custom. They must be on the fringe of the one great soul, for Marco looked up through the Monarchs and the tree of life and he could see the sky. Their sky. A storm was coming. What should he do? Should he wake Mariposa from the reality of her dreams? Think, Marco, think. But Marco was very tired. Perhaps they had a little time. The wind picked up a little. Marco closed his eyes and entered Mariposa's dream. "Dreams are the only real thing."

Butterfly in the Beyond
Beyond Orange

Inside the great butterfly soul, dreaming, Mariposa kept returning to this thought: not even sex was supposed to feel this good. This was beyond sex; it was beyond everything. Beyond orange, beyond Mexico, both the real Mexico and the Mexico of her childhood fairy tales. Beyond sweet, beyond bright, beyond warm. Beyond the blue of not-knowing, beyond knowing and not-knowing. This was beyond the question of knowing, beyond anything cerebral or thinkable, and beyond feeling. Beyond senses, beyond orgasms, beyond self. Mariposa, dreaming, which was the only real thing.

Mariposa, fluttering orangely amid endless orangeness. Mariposa, dreaming. And, yes, her sweet Marco was there, curled against her. He was with her inside the great butterfly soul.

"It's so incredible," Marco was saying, "to be inside this moment with you."

Mariposa sighed. She reached for him, kissed him. This kiss, the moment—these were two things she would be able to live inside of, at least partly, for forever. Neither the kiss nor the moment Marco spoke of, or even him speaking of it, would ever end.

Marco was here with her, but in a way, he had been with her all along.

"I have been with you all along." It was Marco, but Mariposa, inside her dream, their dream, could not tell where his voice was coming from. It seemed to come from everywhere, and from nowhere.

The world was folding into Mariposa, into them, and yet, it was more than the world, or at least, not the world in the very limited sense with which Mariposa had once known it. The world, and beyond—the everything—was at once larger than Mariposa ever could have believed and also, finally, something she could know, could touch. Mariposa, Marco, together: they were everything.

"I'm so glad I found you," she said. But that wasn't right. He had found her. And yet, that wasn't quite right either.

On this point Marco, who was oh so clever—-the quickest cloud-sentence diagrammer, besides the spider, in her long-ago class—but naïve, was uncharacteristically astute on that point.

"We have found," he said, "each other."

Sweet, suddenly wise Marco. And now, Mariposa began to relax into their shared dream. The forever-dream, which turned backwards, from the Beginning of Everything and wheeled forward, too, to The End. Both of which met here, in Times Squared…and thus, didn't exist at all.

Mariposa said, "It doesn't exist at all."

And Marco understood. "Yes."

She felt the universe in the tips of her wings—wings that didn't even really exist anymore, and a universe that had changed completely—and now, she and Marco, dissolved into the real reality, stretched and swirled and expanded, non-physically.

"This is realer than real." Mariposa, bodiless, was nonetheless dizzy. "Oh," she said.

"It's all right," Marco said. "Everything is okay."

"I love you," she said, simply, and so it was—simple. She was startled by how easy it was, this love, and though she had said it before, and meant it, it meant a whole new thing now. This new love expanded, along with everything else, to meet both the beginning and the end, which no longer existed, and to fill up the new, expanded real of this new, dream-only life.

"Yes," Marco said. Because he knew. He knew exactly what she meant. He kissed her, and they continued the this-is-better-than-sex sex.

"Oh, god. Oh, god. Oh, god." Mariposa was off, quivering with her new whole-soul, soul-universe-style orgasm, but Marco hushed her.

"Shh," he said. And Mariposa understood: he didn't want her screams to wake them from this dream, which was the only real thing.

Mariposa could not be hushed, though—she tried, she did—and, abruptly, just as she was in the throes of an orgasm that would have stopped the heart of most creatures, they awoke. Mariposa's orgasm continued. It was the longest yet, and she couldn't stop it if she wanted to, and even though she had slipped over into the non-real of waking, where everything appeared cartoonish and shallow, and the orgasm had lost its super-existential boundlessness, still: how could she will it to end? It went on and on, Mariposa shuddered inside Marco's arms while the less-real-than-dream-real sky stirred, black and gray and purple, above them. Marco was much affected by Mariposa's orgasm. He had always enjoyed it, holding tight to the spazzing Mariposa, but an added benefit of their new heights of love and soul-awareness was that he, too, experienced Mariposa's orgasm. They were inside that orgasm, the one that kept going and going and going, together, and Marco, unused to such intensity, could not speak. Instead, he made a kind of gurgling sound: the sound of a forever-devil-stunted tadpole experiencing more pleasure than any sweet little tadpole was meant to experience.

"Holy fucking god," Marco said at last.

They were awake now, and finally still—no more gurgling or gyrating or shuddering—and a terrible black wind, gritty and blinding, engulfed them. They clung tight to each other, but Mariposa, in the confusion, in the sudden, drenching rain, the savage wind whose howls filled her tiny butterfly ears forcefully, assaultingly, let go of the Tree of Life. Mariposa and Marco were launched out of the great butterfly soul in a massive upsurge which pushed them higher and higher until they were in the thinnest part of the storm, above the wind. The rain still crashed down on them, and Mariposa's sodden wings were sealed together, and she strained to separate them. Marco clung clumsily to her middle-section—they had been unprepared for flight and he was not in his usual flying position. The two hung perilously just above the densest winds, Mariposa's wings growing heavier with rain with every second.

Mariposa, though, still partly living inside that moment, their moment, which would defy the obstacle of time by continuing to beat on, a tiny, persistent thing inside both hers and Marco's hearts, inside their dream. Their moment— the moment they would live inside of for now on—beat outwards, throughout the reaches of the universe, the material one and the nonmaterial one, the universe Mariposa so recently could feel in the tips of her wings. Even now, because of that forever-theirs moment, Mariposa was happy. She and Marco could settle this way, unable to fly, on the surface of the storm for forever, as far as she was concerned.

Oh, she thought, because the wind was too violent for Marco to hear her if she merely spoke aloud, I am so happy.

Me, too, came Marco's thoughts, responding to hers. Me happy, too. Which was strange, because Marco, young as he was, as inclined to speaking, after the Blues took him, in that ridiculous gibberish, at least knew how to use the nominative form of the first person pronoun, singular. And, Marco knew how to use a simple being verb. Plus, his voice, silent as it was, the voice of his thoughts, sounded strained, as if he were working hard, though this might just have been the voice of a tadpole being tossed upon the surface of a storm, using every last bit of strength he had just to hold on.

Crazy happy, Mariposa thought.

Crazy happy, Marco agreed. Now, the strain in his voice was unmistakable. Marco, winded, even in his thought-voice.

What's wrong? Mariposa asked, but before she could complete her thought, she felt the pain—the pain—flare suddenly and forcefully across her back. It reached around and enveloped her abdomen, and she cried out.

She thought: The babies!

In the ecstasy of their oh-so-happy-to-be-having-babies-sex, coupled with oh-so-existentially-complete-inside-the-butterfly-soul-this-is-better-than-sex sex, Mariposa had forgotten all about the actual babies. Babies, Mariposa thought. Did she even want to have babies?

She was so caught up on her pain, and in anxious thoughts about her impending motherhood, Mariposa hardly noticed they were moving higher and eastward, toward the great, blazing sun. They were above the clouds now, and the rain disappeared. Everything was blue.

Mariposa cried, not the cry of pleasure or of physical pain, but of sadness. She had never pictured herself as somebody's mother, and now, the prospect of not just having babies, but a hundred babies, and not just ordinary butterflies, but tadpole-butterfly mutant babies.

She sobbed.

Her mother had been right all along. She had told her not to trust in any of her dreams. Not Broadway. Not Mexico. She would have been right about this, too, if she had known. She would have never have approved of this—the situation Mariposa now found herself in. And not just because of the bizarreness—and probably, Mariposa relented, the ugliness—of the babies, but the whole relation-ship. A butterfly and a tadpole?

Maybe her mother would have been right?

Oh, no, Mariposa, no. It was Marco's thought-voice. It's not true. There was a pause. Marco was still holding onto Mariposa's middle—not the most comfortable of positions for either one of them, especially with Mariposa's mid-section tightening—as hard as a rock—every two minutes or so: butterfly contractions. Horrible. Wretched. This entire situation…

What you're thinking isn't true. Marco. The sky was blue and perfect now, all the gray beneath them, and though they moved slowly, very slowly, Mariposa, whose wings were still stuck together, sealed with rain water, sensed it: they were moving. No longer up, but still, closer, closer to the sun. The horrible clenching came again, and Mariposa bore down against it. She simply wanted to go back. Back, to before the storm, which had snatched her away from such a wonderful place: the butterfly soul, Marco. But she could find no comfort in that memory now. She just wanted to go back, back, to before that. Before Mexico. Before the easy jet stream flight that had carried them there. Before the winery, where she'd been forced to take on the personage of Marilyn Merlot, where Marco had turned blue and weird-talking. Before that, before that first boozy encounter near the goldenrod bush. Before she'd ever compelled any young pupil to look up, consider the clouds.

No, Mariposa. Marco was still speaking-thinking haltingly, as if the strain of simply holding onto her was too much. We belong together, Marco's silent, winded, voice.

Now, the air was warm and dry, the storm growing smaller and smaller beneath them, already beginning to dissipate. Mariposa was recovering from another paralyzing contraction, and everything was finally still and calm enough for her to notice that Marco was not simply holding onto her, allowing the wind to carry them wherever it wanted to carry them. Marco was moving. He was turning the lower half of his little tadpole body in circles. Marco, oddly blue, naïve, who had once rescued them by sprouting arms, was propelling them. He had been working like hell the whole time, steering them out of danger. It had been Marco who had lifted them out of the storm, and Marco who now was moving them toward the sun.

Marco, who had found her.

You beautiful little slimy slug, Mariposa thought, and if she could have repositioned herself, and if she weren't in the middle of laying-eggs-labor, she would have climbed on top of her sweet Marco and lavished all of her appreciation and contrition—I can't believe I questioned you, I questioned us, for a second!—all over him and his eager and magnificent Marco Tad Polo tadpole.

And now, he was explaining something to her. Everything was calm and quiet enough now that he could speak aloud if he wanted to, but he instead continued to think to her. Because, still, even awake in this not-real life, he could. They were forever this way now.

We are this way forever, Marco thought-spoke. We are flying into the sun. Like Daedalus. Something was dawning on Marco now. He sounded a bit panicked. Daedalus: nine, peninsula: dead.

Marco? He wasn't making any sense.

Wheels are circles. Circles are wheels. They were flying right into the great orange-yellow circle of the sun.

Marco?

He had quit propelling and now relaxed his poor little tadpole body, possessing barely enough strength to hold on to Mariposa. Daedalus: nine, peninsula: dead, he thought spoke, weakly. Now that he was no longer working the lower half of his little tadpole body like a propeller, a soft, benevolent wind yet carried them, but they were beginning to dip a bit lower in the sky. The tip of Marco's sluggy body touched a cloud, and Mariposa, out of instinct, lifted her still-stuck-together wings.

Dead, Marco thought-spoke, and when Mariposa, alarmed at the desperation in his voice, looked down, she found fear in Marco's little tadpole eyes. Dead, he said again, hardly able to think-speak at all anymore.

"Oh, no," Mariposa said out loud. She thought it and spoke it: she wanted to be sure he heard her, even if it meant he heard her double: he had to hear her. They were falling now with greater speed, falling through the clouds, which were no longer storm clouds, but beautiful white cumulus clouds, fair weather clouds, wandering clouds. Poor Marco, who was so physically exhausted that he was mentally confused, who believed he had propelled them, with his little tadpole propeller, too high, who feared they were flying into the sun, like Icarus, the son of Daedalus, who didn't realize they were actually plummeting now, through the thin air, that they were now much more likely to die a parched and messy death, crashing into the Mexican desert now hurtling toward them.

"Marco, you sweet and stupid little fuck. We are not going to die at all today. I'm a fucking butterfly, you wonderful dumbass slug." And with that, even though a new contraction wrapped itself around the entirety of her abdomen and lower body, she strained her wing muscles, and, after a moment of two of struggle, as they continued their now-terrifyingly-swift descent, they opened and Mariposa lifted them up at the very last moment. The tip of Marco's sluggy body brushed against the rock-hard parched desert ground.

A moment later, and Mariposa landed them safely, expertly—though Mariposa was not such a great pilot in flight, she could land as gracefully and smoothly as any other butterfly—in a desert that looked so much like a desert, it was almost cartoonish, complete with tumbleweed and cacti. The sun, which they had almost flown into, was a great orange circle beating mercilessly down on them.

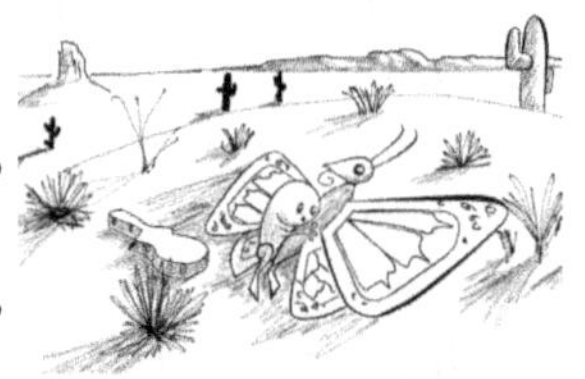

Gracefully and smoothly...

"Mariposa! Mariposa! We're alive!"

Marco had recovered from his exhaustion and fear and was now both thinking and speaking aloud without a trace of tiredness or apprehension. Mariposa could tell by the way he touched her shoulder and slid his little tadpole hand up the length of her side that he had thank-god-we-didn't-burn-up-in-the-sun-or-crash-in-the-desert sex in mind, but Mariposa, who no longer felt as though her body was going to be crushed under the strength of her ever-tightening contractions, now felt an overwhelming need to rid her body of the hundred or so eggs inside of her. She perched rigidly on a piece of dry tumble-weed and cried out. Something was wrong. Something was very wrong.

"Something is wrong," Marco said. He knelt beside her, but she was so focused on her desire to lay her motherfucking eggs that she could not even turn her head to look at him.

"I...need...milkweed," she panted, so softly she was inaudible.

But Marco could hear her thoughts. "Oh, my dear Mariposa, my darling, of course, right away..." but he was stammering, stalling for time. All around them, nothing but cacti and tumbleweed and a few, very few, scrubby bushes.

Think, Marco, think, she heard him think to himself.

Mariposa cried. She couldn't hold out much longer. If she lay her eggs here, they would die. Some things a butterfly just knows. She could not hold out any longer. Her babies, mutants though they were, would die.

Poor, sweet Marco, who could not think of anything else to do, took his guitar case off his squishy tadpole shoulder, and unzipped it. He brought his guitar out and began to play.

Marco. Marco Polo. Mariposa Butterfly.

He thought he might go solo. Until he looked up at the sky.

Mariposa was a Monarch. Marco was a tadpole.
They looked the same in the dark. And with love you never know.

With love you never know. It's one thing then it's two.
And just when you're letting go. Something holds on to you.
So with love you never know.

And Marco understood Mariposa.
And Mariposa was not easy to understand.
She liked Vodka and Mimosas.
And she flew with no idea where they would land.

Mariposa fell in love with the tadpole. She called him her little slug.
And they flew away to lands untold. Where they would not be bugged.

Mariposa liked to sing at the Karaoke bar.
That's where we met, recalled Marco.
A Broadway singer is what she wanted to be.
But she sang like Yoko Ono.

Mariposa Butterfly. Marco. Marco Tad Polo.
It is one thing to be you and I. And with love you never know.

Mariposa heard the music, though distantly. Marco played and played, and Mariposa, who was so focused on her pain and her worry that she could only distantly realize that he had stopped playing and she couldn't hear at all the whop-whop-whop of the helicopter when it descended from the hard blue desert sky. Nor did she feel the sudden, sand-stinging wind generated by its propellers. But she heard Marco's thoughts when a creature emerged and hopped down to the ground: It's the goddamn devil.

"Don't stop on my account," the devil-rabbit said. "Lovely, just lovely."

But Marco had stopped. And now, he stood up to face the devil-rabbit. And Mariposa, who couldn't stand it one more second, lay a single tadpole-butterfly egg on the hot, dry desert ground.

"I'm sorry to intrude on this touching family moment," the devil-rabbit continued, nodding to Mariposa who was half-limping, half-crawling out of but-terfly-instinct to a piece of green—a cactus. Mariposa truly could not wait any longer; she would have to lay the rest of the eggs here.

"But I am here to collect," the devil-rabbit, looking entirely comfortable even in this heat of the desert sun, in his tweed vest. He smiled, jovially. "Tell, me, Bozo Boy, have you done it? Have you discovered the secret of the great butterfly soul?"

And the last thing Mariposa heard before she finished laying her eggs and fell asleep, was her sweet Marco's desperate thoughts: Think, Marco, think, he instructed himself. Think, Marco, think, he told himself again, before opening his sweet little tadpole mouth to speak.

Marco Under Milkweed

Mariposa had saved them. Her wet wings had parted and she had awoken from the trance of the one great soul to save their one great life. Now they made "near-death-experience-love" in the morning desert air, but Marco knew Mariposa was about to have her babies—their babies. He thought hard. To himself. Unlike limited humans, when two insects, or an insect and an amphibian fall in love and their love has fallen in love, and their falling in love has fallen in love, they can begin to communicate telepathically. So somewhere in that violent storm that killed many thousand monarchs and nearly killed Marco and Mariposa, and the wind howled and blew them upward toward the sun, they began to think/speak.

Now they had landed and were safe for the moment. Marco was having trouble distinguishing Mariposa's thought/speech from her speech/speech. Mainly because Mariposa talked a lot, so her speech/speech and her thought/speech made her even more incomprehensible than usual. It was like the Tower of Babel without the tower.

"Marco, I have to have my babies soon (speech). You have to do something (thought). Why is he looking that way (thought) We need Milkweed and we need it quickly (speech)."

Marco stared blankly but did not answer because he thought it was her thought/speech. "Marco, answer me. Are you listening?"

"Oh yes. Sorry. I thought it was your thought/speech. We need to close down the thought channel for now. It's too confusing. I need to focus on the thought/action channel."

"We need Milkweed. Or our babies will die."

Marco looked out across the parched, pale desert where they had landed. Cacti was the only plant he could see. Just then a noise from above broke the desert silence and a helicopter landed near them and the devil rabbit stepped out. "Yo Bozo boy. Tell me all about the secrets of the great soul. I see you found your Mariposa. Hey, do you like my ride. It's a helicopter. Get it, Hell-i-coptor."

"Quick Devil. There's no time to lose. Put some water on to boil. Go get a warm wash cloth. Mariposa is about to have her babies. Then get in your helicopter, and go fetch some Milkweed…Then I will tell you all about the one great soul." Marco seemed delirious.

Marco then went to his guitar case and opened it. He pulled out a book and began turning through it quickly.

"Marco, oh Marco what are you doing? I can't hold them back much longer. What are you reading?"

"The Guide to Flora and Fauna. There has to be some kind of Milkweed that grows around here. I picked it up when we first got together. I stole it from the bookbugmobile." He turned the pages frenetically. "Here. Desert Milkweed. Grows in the Sonoran desert of Northern Mexico. Nectar rich. Can communicate telepathically with some types of butterflies.

"Quick Mariposa. Turn on your thought/speech again. Raise your antenna. Maybe there's some nearby."

"Okay, I'll try, but the pain is getting worse."

Marco put on his little aviator cap. He had made fake antennae with some guitar strings and aluminum foil, and with his little mechanical mind he had gotten them to work. He could pick up insect baseball games and insect radio stations, and now he hoped it might pick up the telepathic musings of Milkweed plants.

The devil stood deviantly, mockingly, musing over the frantic scene. Mariposa writhing in her beautiful colorful pain. The pain of birth he could never know. The one great soul he had been kicked out of for being a horny little devil. The heroic innocence of Marco in his little aviator cap, creatively saving them until the next crisis emerged.

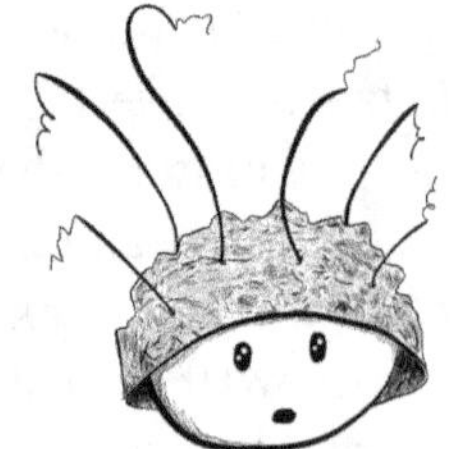

...guitar strings and aluminum foil...

"Oh what fools these insects be…Oh honey pole, can you pick up some Milkweed at the supermarket on your way home?" the devil said mockingly. "Marco, do you know how many tadpoles it takes to screw in a light bulb?" The devil rabbit grinned.

Marco hated tadPolish jokes. Marco hated the devil. Marco no longer feared the devil because the one great soul had given him the secret, the secret power that would neutralize the devil. He could already see through it. That the devil was jealous and envious and spiteful and unhappy. His glibness and cleverness and his ability to party endlessly was just a facade and a ruse. The devil was a ruser. And Marco did the thing the devil hated most. Marco ignored him.

He ran over to Mariposa. "Try to hold on. Here read about the milkweed and all the nectar they produce and I'll be right back. Hold on."

"I'll try, Marco. I'll try…I hear something, Marco. Over that rise. Do you see the large cactus there. It's coming from over there. Please hurry."

Marco adjusted his fake antenna to see if he could catch anything…All he could get was a Mexican soap opera.

"Do you know how many tadpoles it takes to adjust rabbit ears," the devil rabbit wiggled his own ears.

Without hesitation Marco ran on his own feeble legs over the rise toward the large cactus tree whose top was only visible from where they had landed. Once he topped the sandy parched hill and reached the cactus tree he could see other vegetation that towered over him. He listened. The Mexican soap opera droned on. He ripped off his aviator cap and listened again.

"Listen, Marco listen," Marco said aloud which was his custom. He heard it faintly but close by. Not words, but a soft humming, like music, but softer somehow. Like "The Flight of the Bumblebee" played by fairies. Like music a tadpole or a butterfly, or a combination of the two, might hear in a dream. The dream of music. If music dreamed.

And there it was. Marco recognized it from the picture from "Flora and Fauna," the Desert Milkweed. And he could see other milkweed plants as well, and they were all dream humming, their dream music and if Mariposa could lay her eggs in this symphony of sound, this home of hum, so imperceptible that only dream creatures could hear it, then their babies might be saved.

But there was no time to waste. It had taken Marco a long time to walk over the rise to find the plants and now he had to run back to Mariposa. He listened for her thought/speech, and he could only hear the shrill static of pain.

"Okay, Milkweed. Don't go anywhere. I'll be back with Mariposa. Boil some water. Get everything ready. From here to maternity. The incredible gurney."

Marco was still a bit delirious with fear and excitement. He ran as fast as he could. He would have to somehow get Mariposa to fly. Would she be able to? He did not know. She would have to. He tried to reach her by thought/ speech, but got an out-of-order message: "The number you are trying to reach is out of service at this time."

When he reached Mariposa, she was barely conscious. "Mariposa, Mariposa. I found it. Did you hear me? I found it! You'll have to fly us there."

Mariposa opened her beautiful dream-filled butterfly eyes and looked at Marco with a look that melted the poor tadpole's heart. "I can't, Marco. I'm sorry, Marco. I couldn't wait. I'm dying, Marco. Let me go. I don't want you to see me die."

Then Marco saw it. All around Mariposa were at least a hundred eggs. Dead. Stillborn in the hot sand of the desert.

Then the devil piped up. "Do you know how many tadpoles it takes to scramble an egg? Oh don't worry about the mess. I'll clean it up."

Then something strange happened, that could only happen in the case of such hopelessness. Instead of feeling sadness, and such terrible loss, and sorrow, Marco felt hope, and resolve, and courage in the face of the worst sorrow he had ever felt. That any tadpole had ever felt, he thought.

"Think, Marco, think." He looked at his guitar case as if it were a treasure chest. And then he remembered the concoction Blind Catfish Walking had given him to stop his maturation. To freeze him in that state between tadpole and frog, that had allowed Mariposa to love him forever. He consulted his mental almanac, and it was not the end of forever. The almanac said so. So that settled that. He went to his guitar case, pushed the devil out of the way, got him in a short headlock, gave him a nookie, and grabbed the little vial of fluid, that was part nectar, part bourbon, part ginseng, part milkweed. He held it to Mariposa lips and she drank reluctantly.

"Come on, Mariposa. drink. You have to drink. Forever is not over yet. The almanac says so, and you don't want to go against the almanac, do you? There might be more babies. You may not be finished. It may be like your orgasms. They just keep on coming."

She drank. She heard him. She opened her eyes wide and felt the liquid flow through her abdomen and then to her wings, and finally to her heart. Her wings spread in all their fading beauty.

"Come on, Mariposa. One more sip. Drink it all because sometimes all the magic potion is at the bottom…Come on. That's it…You don't want this to be your karaoke swan song. I have a cigarette for you after this is over. Think about it, Mariposa, a cigarette."

She drank the last bit like the old Mariposa. Like it was a shot of nectar infused bourbon. She looked at Marco and spoke softly but with the old bitchiness that Marco had come to love so much.

"You are one fucking amazing tadpole, Marco Tad Polo. I love you," and she kissed him.

"Hold that thought," she said. "Climb on my back… easy… okay." And Mariposa flapped her wings and they rose unsteadily and flew just above the sand and rocks. Sometimes so low that Marco maneuvered himself so when they scraped he could push off with his feet.

They came over the rise and Marco whispered. "A little higher, Mariposa, just a little higher." There. Hear it. The dream music."

And Mariposa fluttered up with the last bit of her strength and they landed softly on the leaf of the milkweed. Marco whispered again. "Now, Mariposa. Are there more babies? The Milkweed maternity staff has arrived."

"Give her a nectar epidural. An emergency B-section," the Milkweed spoke. "Let's make her comfortable. We'll put her in a butterfly coma once we get her attached to the underside of the leaf. You can wait up here on top. It will be night soon. Great star gazing. There's nectar brownies there by the stem. We'll take care of the rest," and with that the milkweed took Mariposa away.

Marco sat down on top of the leaf, grabbed a nectar brownie and took a bite. It would be a long wait. He leaned back and looked out over the late afternoon desert. Desert mountains rose up in the distance. He dared to dream that they might just be safe for a while and Mariposa would lay her eggs and be fine.

"I've almost come full circle," he said aloud as was his custom. He thought back and tried to recognize the young tadpole who had started this journey.

It was difficult. But he did think of the kindness of the milkweed and how he understood its language of music and soft murmurs. It allowed him to remember the tadpole deities he had known in his tadchildhood at the pond. How there were two things in the beginning. The moss and the algae. He had learned this in sedimentary school.

"In the beginning there was the Moss and the Algae. And they were brothers. One ruled the soft quiet banks, and one ruled the stillness of the pond. 'What's it all about Algae? Is it just for the moment we live?' And I wonder about my old friend the Dung Beetle, the star gazer who taught me to look at the stars and told me stories about the Moss. Moss Heart. Ah, I hope my old friend is okay. I think about all the old friends I will never see again, but at least I can remember them now. How strange. How far I've come. How far we've come. The becoming and the begoing."

And he thought of Mariposa sleeping, dreaming in a coma suspended beneath a leaf above the ground, and how he loved her above all things. "What's it all about, Algae?"

"Nice view, huh," the Devil Rabbit appeared above him. "Is your lady laying some more eggs?"

"We don't know, the Milkweed is taking care of her. They've put her in a coma. Want a brownie?"

"Nice try, Tadpole. But they're poisonous to rabbits, even devil ones."

"If you take her eggs, are they then deviled eggs."

"Ah, the road to hell is paved with bad comedians. I'm growing tired of all this. I don't like this desert. I'm going to Las Vegas where there are no tadpoles or milkweed. Did you find the secret of 'the One Great Soul?'"

"I did." Marco put the devil in a Half Nelson (tadpoles excel in wrestling). Now that Marco understood that the devil was a fraud just like the Lizard of Ooze, he wasn't afraid of him anymore.

"Pray, do tell me and you'll be free of me for a while, a long while… I need to be around humans. Humans in Las Vegas where sin is taken seriously and treated with the respect that it deserves." The devil rabbit spoke through clenched rabbit teeth.

"The secret is there is no secret. It's just a place. A place where a million monarchs gather. And the secret is, is that it is more than one thing. There's a city inside and Times Squared, and you can spell things forward and backward. And you can take a guided tour and there's a gift shop, but in the end, it's a scam. A tourist trap. It's all about what you bring to the encounter. There's no secret. It's like you, a scammer, a trickster, a ruser. Devil never even lived."

"What did you say?" The devil said as Marco let him free after applying the Full Nelson.

And for the first time, the devil looked scared. "Who told you to say that?" The devil was apparently having a real Rumpelstiltskin moment. He stomped and twirled around like a Tadmanian Devil. "No! No! No! No!" And the devil rabbit stomped up so much dust that he stomped himself right back into the ground which disappointed Marco a little because he was ready to dropkick the devil right into a cactus. But maybe this time the Devil Rabbit would be gone for good.

"Nobody told me, Devil. It's just a palindrome. Spelled the same forward and backwards. Just like you, it doesn't mean anything. Just like you, it swallowed itself… It reminds me of a story the dung beetle told me once about a snake who started eating this huge frog by sneaking up behind it and biting it on its behind, and as he was swallowing him, the snake swished his tail in front of the half swallowed frog, so the frog bit the snake's tail and hung on and started eating the snake. They both kept eating each other. First one would get ahead and then the other would seem to get ahead and after a while, all that was left of the frog was its lips and all that was left of the snake was its head. Then they both took one big gulp and they both disappeared."

Marco stopped and looked out at the first stars and chuckled the way bad comedian tadpoles do. "That's just the way life is."

As the night deepened, Marco lost track of tadpole time. The nectar brownie had mellowed him into a tadpuddle of introspection. As he reclined in the leaf lounge chair, half asleep and half awake, and half something else (two halves and one halve not) a bug landed softly on the roof of the leaf and sat down beside Marco. Marco glanced at the bug who was now looking at the magazines.

"Why are all the magazines six months behind in hospital waiting rooms?"

Marco sat up and started to say something, but the bug continued. "The Milk Weeder's Digest. What a ragweed publication that is. really? The New York Review of Bugs, they could do better. And, look, The Farmer's Almanac. Who the hell reads that anymore?"

Marco smiled. A nectar brownie smile.

"Hi. You're a tadpole if I'm not mistaken. What is a tadpole doing up on a milkweed leaf?"

"Long story. Long, long story," Marco spoke quietly and looked out at the talkative bug through his half closed eyes. "My lover, a Monarch butterfly, is trying to have babies. I sold my soul to the devil so I could remain a mutant tadpole. We just got blown out of the "one great soul" by a storm and now the devil wants the babies, and we escaped to this milkweed plant. Any questions?" Marco spoke in a world-weary voice. He didn't even know if the bug, a stink bug he presumed, was real or not. His reality now had been reduced to forms and shadows. "Dreams are the only real thing," he said aloud.

"Wow. So it's true. I read a story like this once in The National Enquirer and when I got the call. I couldn't believe it," the bug stared at Marco, bug-eyed.

"Who are you?" Marco asked in a way as if he really didn't care. "You're a Stinkbug, right? I knew a Dung Beetle once who told me about the stars. The Big

Dumpster, The Milky Weed."

"I'm not a Stink bug, at least not anymore. I worked for the Pest Office for a while, delivering mail. But I got a promotion and became a Stork Bug. I deliver babies and eggs. I'm bringing you your babies, well, they're eggs. I just dropped them off downstairs. You have to sign for them though… Yeah, I've known a dung beetle or two. Solitary and contemplative souls. Funny. You wouldn't think. One told me a story once," and the Stork Bug looked up at the Milky Weed and began his story:

"In the beginning, there was just muck and mud and all was formless, and the stars were in the heavens and the group of stars I call the Big Dumpster dropped an egg into the muck. From the egg came all life, but it was the small stuff, bacteria, and amoebas, and little fishes, and sperm, and even tadpoles, and the largest creature to emerge from the egg was the chicken, so when someone asks you which came first, the chicken or the egg, well, now you know. Anyway, the chickens multiplied and flourished, and actually everything was flourishing. There was a whole lot of flourishing going on, over flourishing. So creatures were evolving and morphing like hot crab cakes. Snakes and frogs and alligators and catfish and cats and lions and tigers were springing out of the muck. It was quite the orgy. But in the begatting the twin muckers, Algae and Moss who had been there from the beginning, said this is getting out of hand and asked sky to calm things down a bit. So sky held off the rain for a while so the multiplying stopped just in time because there were some weird things happening like the wedgie fish and hippopossumus. Then in the chicken capital there was an egg about to hatch in the back of a coop de ville because there was no room in the front seat. Chicken worshipers from all over came and when the chicken hatched, it was an ostrich, and all the worshippers were sorely disappointed."

"That's one ugly chicken," said all the important chickens who were there. And they claimed he was the devil's chicken and they performed an ostrichcism. That didn't work so they did an extraostracism.

"That's still one ugly chicken," they said, so they exiled him into the Out-black. And because of the extreme blackness and the ostrich's long neck, he had a perfect view of the stars that no one else could see. Except the kangaroos. And I have no idea where I was going with this story, but that's the whole point or most of the whole point and don't you forget it."

"Are you saying my babies will be ugly?"

"No. I'm saying they will be the most beautiful babies ever born because you will teach them the story of the Dung Beetle and the stars in the same story… You know, we all live in the same story." As the Stork Bug said this, he handed Marco a piece of paper. "Here sign this… It's been nice talking to you, but life goes on and on and on and I have a lot of deliveries to make. Mayflies are getting it on as we speak. Preying Mantis are having babies and eating their mates. Hey, be glad you're not a male mantis."

Marco signed the paper and then turned it over and examined it closely. "No fine print is there?"

"Nope. They're your babies now. No returns, though. No going back is there?"

"Nope. No going back… Can I see them?"

"Don't know," said Stork Bug standing. "I'm just the deliverer. Fine with me. Give them a kiss, hope they come out all right. I'm no doctor either. Stay here. Look at the Milky Weed. You'll know… I think I'll take a brownie with me. Adieu." The Stork Bug then lifted his wings and flew off into the desert night.

Butterfly in the Dark

Marco? Marco? Are you there? Oh, please say you are there, or rather, here. Here, with me, somehow, because it's dark in here. Wherever here is. It's dark, but warm and floaty. (I like floaty.) I feel okay, I feel better than okay—very very floaty, plus swirly and a little swimmy and warm—but I also don't feel okay. Not okay at all because I'm alone in here, in this here I don't know at all.

Marco? Marco? Are you there? Can you hear me?

The last time I was alone in a dark warm place was when I was just a girl, wrapped up in my cocoon. A girl becoming a woman. That was a different kind of alone, and a different kind of dark. I was held snug in that dark place, and it was the first time I experienced anything like the Great Butterfly Soul, because I was there, becoming. My wings—my very butterflyness—were knitting themselves into my hard black spine. I didn't know precisely what was happening, but I knew I was growing, becoming the kind of creature I was meant to be.

Do you know what that's like, Marco? To feel yourself becoming the creature you know, deep in your heart of hearts, that you are supposed to be?

But now, I feel stopped, somehow. Still. Too still. Swirly and swimmy, but still. Like some kind of a buzzing, so constant, and so there from the very beginning, I never noticed it before. I never really even heard it before at all.

That buzzing, however small, almost unhearable, has stopped, and now, the silence is huge. I can't hear these words, as I think them, transmute them, or try to, to you, to my dear sweet slug, The silence is too huge.

I fear I am unbecoming…Is such a thing possible? Will I lose my wings?

I was something at the Chicken and Egg Pub. I was somebody there.

Marco? Are you there? Don't tell me you're off with that damn rabbit. You and your devil.

Cooking up some new plan…

Oh, god, Marco. The babies. My babies. Where are my babies?

Where are you?

Are we all dead? Is that what this is?

****

Oh Mariposa, Mari, Posa, Monarcha butterfly, the words sing to me like thoughts, but words are not thoughts. I love you, but "I love you" is just words for the indescribable feeling. Feeling mixed with the experience of intimacy. Of touching, of flying, of sharing the secrets of a life, of making life out of love, and love out of life, and then reducing it to three words, "I love you." So totally inadequate to where we have been, to where we are going. Where are we going?

Where have we been?

Yes. I can hear you. Barely. Softly. Intertwined with the so-soft music of the Milkweed. Lullabying us in this lulling place. Lulla, lulla, lulla-bye. This place that is nowhere and everywhere. I am with you but not with you. But I will find you. I can only make out some of the words. I hear the word "slug." I don't like the word "slug." It sounds too much like "thug" or "lug" , but I like the word "bug" and "rug" is fine, and I love the word "hug," but "slug" sounds heavy like a weight we can barely bear. If you build a house where each side of the house has a southern exposure and a bear wanders by outside. What color is the bear? What color is the bear, Mariposa? If we can answer that maybe we'll be saved.

"Slug" is a word too heavy like "anchor" or "bowling ball" and we need lightness, words that fly through this darkness like beams of lightness. Like floaty, like swimmy, like swirly. Words that wrap around us like a cocoon, like a chrysalis. No slug trail, but a shooting star trail that leads us onto sky roads, happy trails, happy trails to you. Words sing to me. Trails onto trails. Long and winding roads. Follow the yellow brick road. Scared Crow. Why can't I remember being born, Mariposa? Water. Swimmy, swirly, floaty. Being born one thing only to become another, only to want to be what one already is, but having to change to stay the same. Becoming and begoing. Roads lead onto roads. Dreams lead on to dreams.

Where are you, Mariposa? I can hear you. Soul singing, disembodied. Oh how I love your body. Rubbing your antennae, stroking your abdomen, your wetness, swimmy in your wetness, floaty in your kisses, swirly in your winged orgasms. I want that again and again, Mariposa. Forever is not here yet. Remember the almanac. Remember flying in each other's arms. Sleeping on the wind.

Please don't leave me. The silence is large, but the music is soft. And I am on the edge of that silence. Knocking, knocking.

Knock, knock.

Who's there?

Wendy.

Wendy who?

Wendy wind blows the cradle will rock.

I have a cigarette for you. A cigarette Mariposa, a cigarette.

What color is the bear, Mariposa? What color is the bear?

****

Oh my god, a cigarette. I remember those. The smooth, firm paper cylinder, my lips, the tip of my tongue against that perfect cottony circle, oh. And then, the snap of flame, caught on the tobaccoed tip, crinkling around, igniting, and me drawing the smoke into my ready, fluttery butterfly lungs. Sweet toxins, sweet, true flame. Sweet, sweet.

Yes, I hear you, Marco. I don't know what the hell color that stupid fucking bear is, but I hear you, oh, the words, the tiny reedy squeak of my beautiful, sexy, sweet, slimy slug.

Does slug sound heavy to you? And slug trails unpleasant? I love slug. I love the word, I love the meaning. Slug: a surrendering softness. A kiss. Slug: sweet slug. My love. If you were a grommet, a clank, a phlegm, a yeast, a discharge, a lurch, I would love you and I would love any sound that meant you. I would sing the word inside my head and think of you and wait for you, your answer.

Will you sing for me, my love? My sweet, phlegmy slug? Will you play your tadpole guitar for me?

Will you come to me, on a trail of stars or slime—why should I care which? So long as it brings you to me? I crave your sluggy softness, your Marco-ness... your tadpole. My god, to think of that. Oh, if you were here with me...if we were returned to our bodies...me to my hard black exoskeleton, orgasm-fluttery wings, you swimmy but insistent...hardly slug-soft at all...inside my wetness...

Oh, god. You said cigarette. I heard you say cigarette.

I am remembering now. All the way back to the first cigarette we ever shared. Near the puddle near the path between the pond and my goldenrod home of too many sisters. You thought I was a sweet and caring teacher, pure in my pedagogical and grammarical intentions—diagramming clouds—until you met me on that path and discovered the true me: drunk on bourbon-infused nectar and weepy and horny as hell...

Me, the Queen of Ellipses...do you remember when you used to call me that? Oh. Back in our early days, when you were a virgin in so many ways, untested in the lands of punctuation and unfinished sentences...

Once upon a time, I was a not-yet butterfly inside a dark, unknown cocoon. I had spent my youth munching on leaves and dreaming of the day I would be beautiful.

Where were you then, Marco? Not yet a tadpole, not slimy yet or sweetly sluggy. You weren't even an egg yet, or a twinkle in your father's eye. You simply weren't. Not yet.

And yet, I think I felt you then, bodiless, as I feel you now. You—though I didn't know it yet—were somehow with me then, inside my cocoon, and before... all the days at the other end of our forever...Is that possible? Is it true?

Can remembering what we can't remember—the start before our start— help us find our forever?

Please, no more stupid knock-knock jokes or bear riddles. You, Marco. I want you. You, you miserable sweet sexy slug...

Come to me.

Did I hear you say cigarette?

****

Knock, knock.
Who's there?
Phlegm.
Phlegm who?
Phlegm pickens in here in the out there. The Outblack.
The kangaroo. The boomerang.
Knock, knock.
Who's there.
Yeast.
Yeast who?
Yeast is yeast and west is west. Out there in the in here.

Answer me Mariposa. I have to play all the parts. Knocker and Knockee. I know you don't like knock, knock jokes. Or riddles. But you have to answer the riddle. What color is the bear? Think, Mariposa, think. The riddle. I was there before I was there. You were with me before you were with me. What color is forever? Forever has to start somewhere? Out there. In here.

I remember the first time I saw you. Me, a little tadpole school boy. Feeling frightened and alone among the noisy May Flies and the colorful spiders. Making fun of me. Then I saw you, my teacher, your beautiful wings and body, the very vision of an angel, and I fell in love with that vision, hopelessly, helplessly, while a spider stole my lunch money, and a beetle slapped me on my head. Me a phlegm, a clank, a discharge. And you were in the Out There. In the world bright and beautiful and smart and the thing I wanted but could never have, and I was locked in the In Here. In the slime and muck and you were a creature who had never known the slime and muck. My brothers, Slime and Muck, and don't forget Grommet and Clank, and Phlegm and Lurch.

I didn't even know what Ellipses were. As I watched you diagramming, on the outblack board for the first time, and I heard Ellipses from your lips. I dreamed it was a body part beneath the orangeness of your wings. Soft and forbidden. Knock, knock. Let me in. I thought of kissing your ellipses. Who's there? Algae. Algae who? What's it all about, Algae? Until you told me it meant an omission. Loving you became my omission. Dot Dot Dot. You said I looked like a dash. A fat dash. But dashing. A hint: the bear, dashing through the snow. An omission impossible. You smiled at me. My semi-colon fell. I tripped. Dot dot dot. Remorse code. There was something in your ellipses. A total ellipses. A yearning, a longing. I saw it. I felt it. The spiders were misbehaving. Stupid immature spiders. You pointed at me and said, "Just for that, Marco you stay after class." I replied, "But I didn't do anything."

"Yes, but it's no fun keeping them after class."

And we walked in the sky on the scaffolding of diagrammed sentences and you took me by my little forming hand and led me among the towering flowers. A tower of flowers. And you kissed me. The tip of your tongue finding mine. The feeling of the In Here bursting forth into the Out There, and baby were you out there. No ellipses here. No omission, but O O O, dot, dot, dot. How was I to know you were such a wild woman, no angelly vision, but a slut to a slug. We shared a cigarette. You laughed. I coughed. You fixed me a drink. You laughed. I sputtered. You fondled my prefix. You let me touch your fragment. You called me a virgin. I asked if that was anything like a clank. You said let me show you. You climbed on top of me. I saw God. He was wearing ellipses. And sun glasses. I knew then I was beyond Tadpole hood. I was Marco Tad Polo world traveler, adventurer, lover! I used an Exclamation mark. Premature exclamation.

We diagrammed "forever." It ended with ellipses.

Where is the beginning? I asked. "The beginning is understood," you replied. Actually, you replied, "The fucking beginning is fucking understood, my little bitch of a slug." You had been drinking for a time now, and you were very fond of the word fucking, and so my foul-mouthed angel, I am here, Out There very near the In Here. Remembering what we cannot remember. Finding what everyone told us did not exist. Perfect love. Like the sentence you diagrammed for me in the sky. The perfect sentence. The perfect life. Made out of love, and sky, and slime, and words, and touch and ending with…

****

Okay, you miserable little slug. I'll play.

Knock, knock.
Who's there?
The stupid fucking question about the stupid fucking bear.
The stupid fucking question about the stupid fucking bear, who?
(The bear is white, of course. A house with a southern exposure
from each window sits at the North Pole, so that bear is a polar

bear. And all polar bears are white.
Which proves…?)

Knock, knock.
Who's there?
The color of forever.
The color of forever, who?

That's the way it works. You open up one end of forever and
the other end opens, reaches back and just keeps reaching.
So that meeting you becomes the reason I became a teacher.
So that cloud-diagramming, as a pastime, a discipline, a calling,
was invented solely so that you and I would turn our eyes,
together, into the Out There…
So that the reason the reason for the whole fucking universe
is this: our perfect love.

Knock, knock.
Who's there?
The color of forever is white, like the polar bear.
The color of forever is white, like the polar bear, who?

But we don't know the color. Or, at least, we can't name it. We don't have
the right word. Because what we have, right now, between us, in this dream-
space—the only real thing—is all we have of it.
It's just like how wrong I was to say that ellipses are only about omission.
That's what I used to think. It's the opposite of omission. Those three dots. They
contain everything, every possibility.
Knock, knock.
Who's there?
The color of forever.
The color of forever, who…?
Exactly.

Or, it could be that the color of forever is the color of our babies. Orange
like my wings, like the great butterfly soul, yellow like the desert, tweed like the
rabbit devil you wrestled to the ground, green like you were when I found you,
blue like your blues, the real-deal blues, red like the merlot pond.
Our babies, Marco. Our babies. We are having babies, you and me. There's
our piece of forever right there.

Knock, knock…

Damn it, Marco. Just come in. Just come in, and find me, like you did that day between the pond and the goldenrod bush. Find me, like you did when we nearly crash landed, me with my torn wing, you with your new limbs. Find me, like you did when I, scorched by the terrible great buzzing light, fell to the earth.

Find me, find me, like the first time you ran your little green-blue tadpole hand up and down the length of my exoskeleton. You searching for my ellipsis…

Find me, like we found perfect love. The perfect life. Made out of love, and sky, and slime, and cigarettes, and words, and your guitar and your touch and my touch and ending with…

But it doesn't end. You miserable, beautiful slug, it doesn't.

First you find me, and then, we continue on with our forever.

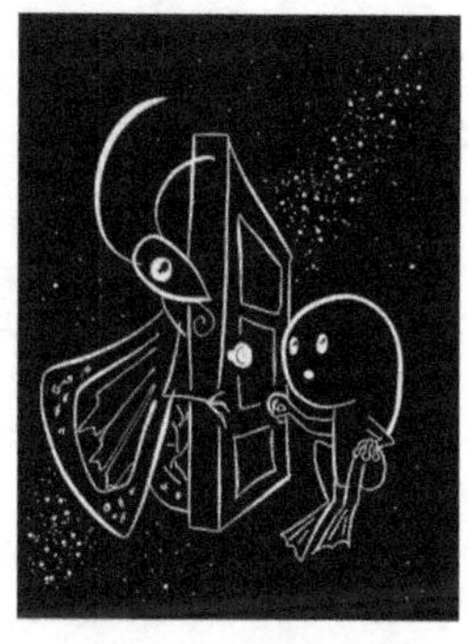

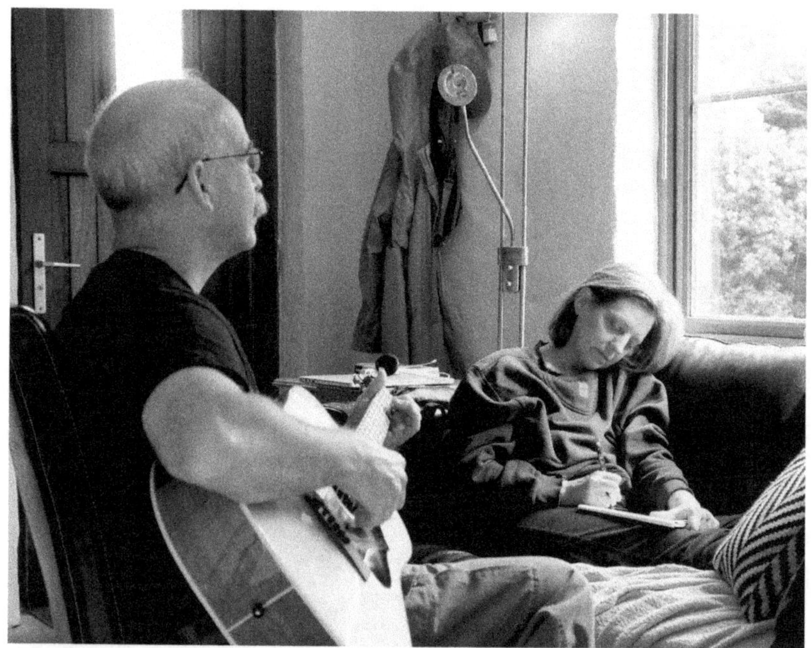

Marcy Lewis is a fiction-writer and a teacher. One of her very favorite things is sitting on the deck at the end of the day with a glass of wine or a beer and her husband. She loves This American Life, Mary Oliver's poetry, Shirley Jackson's short novels, and Aimee Bender's stories. She lives in western North Carolina with her husband, her two children, and a cat named Lucy.

Freddy Bradburn, writing as Freddy Bradburn, is a songwriter, multi-instrumentalist, and retired teacher who lives with his wife, Susan, in Marion, N.C. He has recorded numerous CD's as his closets indicate. He is currently producing a musical play for the Historic Carson House in Marion, and a folk opera for the local community theater. He is also trying to turn their cat Lucy into a dog.